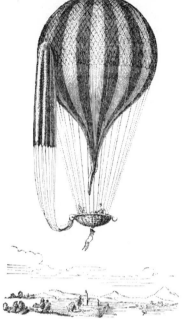

LOWESTOFT CHRONICLE

2011

ANTHOLOGY

LOWESTOFT CHRONICLE

2011 ANTHOLOGY

edited by Nicholas Litchfield

Lowestoft
Chronicle
Press

LOWESTOFT CHRONICLE 2011 ANTHOLOGY

SUBMISSIONS

The editors welcome submissions of poetry, prose, and essays. For submission information, please visit our website at www.lowestoftchronicle.com or email: submissions@lowestoftchronicle.com

Published by Lowestoft Chronicle Press, Cambridge, Massachusetts
www.lowestoftchronicle.com

First Edition: June 2011

Cover by Tara Litchfield

ISBN 13: 978-0-9825365-1-3
ISBN 10: 0-9825365-1-8

Printed in the United States of America

CONTENTS

Editor's Note | Nicholas Litchfield | 7

FICTION

POETRY

CREATIVE NON-FICTION

FLASH FICTION

CONTRIBUTORS | 105

COPYRIGHT NOTES | 110

"If this little book slips out of your Gucci purse and over the side of your gondola, you'll cry less than if it was your precious electronic reading device."

— editor

EDITOR'S NOTE

For the last year or so, we at Lowestoft Chronicle have been confined to a dank office cubicle, squandering daylight hours sifting through thousands of emails from writers, poets, and artists from around the world. Our goal has been to produce an online literary magazine, quarterly, featuring fiction, non-fiction, poetry, and artwork, with an emphasis on travel and a bent for humor. Tens of spools of Scotch Tape and gallons of red ink have gone into the realization of this project. We have hardly had time to do our day jobs; the mammoth stack of papers in our filing tray has had to be transported straight to the shredder rather than filed.

Our first year is over and four seasonal issues of the magazine are behind us. By way of celebration, we have picked through our favorite pieces from the online editions for inclusion in our companion print anthology. In turn, we hope this small softcover tome makes for the perfect travel companion. Presented in the preferred format for reading while seated on a toilet seat, perhaps in an airplane; the ideal weight and size to line the pocket of one's safari jacket on a sightseeing or hunting expedition; substantial enough to fill those dull moments on a whale spotting jaunt on a luxury whaling boat. If this little book slips out of your Gucci purse and over the side of your gondola, you'll cry less than if it was your precious electronic reading device, say a laptop, or Kindle, or iPhone.

With the world going digital, the physical book replaced

by an electronic one, the family vacation replaced by the 'work retreat', it may seem terribly unfashionable of us to persist with a print anthology and, indeed, the out-dated notion of travel for recreational purposes. What can we say? We at the *Chronicle* are dinosaurs. Even our mother's Facebook, Fark, Digg, and Twitter. Boy can they talk!

If petitioning one's overbearing manager for the right to take a one-week vacation this year is too stressful for you, why not unwind with a well-earned weekend visit to the local park with your book of choice—with any luck, this one. Lose yourself in one of the many poems and stories and essays found within these pages. Brinna Deavellar can eloquently describe the exhausting ordeal of attempting to reach the summit of Mount Fuji so you won't have to; immerse yourself in Eric G. Müller's defiant trek across South Africa in order to escape a slipshod haircut by a tyrant headmaster; let Jeremy Rich lead you down the cobbled streets of Prague, and William Doreski take you up the Panama canal; cherish the beauty Lisa Abellera can extract from a weary black and white photograph, and glimpse the future of air travel through Phil Smith III's eyes— an exquisitely beautiful, clothes-free travel experience; and take in Frank Roger's warming apocalyptic vision, where characters are confined to a cave, barely visible by the light of a flickering torch, faced with the knowledge that as soon as they leave their shelter sudden death awaits them.

This is a collection loosely bound by the theme of travel. Sometimes the connection is a tenuous one, like in Tim Conley's comically brilliant "Compassion," where a couple discover a stranger on their doorstep, gagged and tethered to an old cherrywood chair, and debate what they should do with him. Nothing in the story conveys any sense of travel, per se, but certainly the man gagged and bound in the chair has experienced one hell of a journey.

Other stories in this collection may also bear a very loose relation to travel, like Tyke Johnson's "May Prostitutes Only Take Cash," which is an amusing illustration of the perils of shoe shopping for the impulse purchaser armed with a valid credit card and faced with a persuasive Foot Locker salesman named Hunter; or Jennine Capó Crucet's memorable "Photo Club Project," where a discerning teacher carefully assesses the artistic merits of a girl's home photos; or Tom Mahony's "Butts-Up," where we learn of an exciting innovation of the game tennis involving Bud Light and butt cheeks.

The themes explored in this assortment of long and short fiction, poetry, and creative non-fiction, are as broad and varied as a rack of travel brochures in a Thomson's travel agency. And for all the emphasis on travel, there is hardly a beach in sight. Although, Laury A. Egan does manage to find a desolate one in "Point No Point," and Jack Frey leads us past one on the way to a quarrel with a movie star in "The Shooting Party".

In Ron D'Alena's "Sunlight" we are momentarily transported back to 1944, to World War II, and for a moment we find ourselves at a CYO day camp in the 1980's, singing "Tomorrow" from Annie, as in Aida Zilelian's nostalgic "Liar, Liar".

In some stories the location is perhaps less exotic. Gone are the desert and the mountains and the ocean, and instead we find ourselves in Austin, Texas. In "Johnny and Louie" Michael Connor provides a comedian's snapshot journey through the streets of Austin on the way to a few bars, ably escorted by a couple of vagrants; while Katherine Hinkebein's playful "Dented" wills you to the end and makes you wonder why more comedic mileage isn't got out of the RV shower.

In Howard Waldman's "Waiting for the Train" the narrator,

with one foot in the grave, returns to a distant meaningful place of his youth—the railway tracks. While in Michael C. Keith's science fiction story "Magic Skin," Huru Mohubi, the main character, races to his village, pursued by hunters with machetes, hoping to avoid being hacked to death because of the color of his skin. In Davide Trame's "Gout" death has already arrived, with the eagle pecking between ligament and bone.

So, while you pour yourself that Scotch and soda, and light your Cuban cigar, take a moment, or perhaps your entire lunch hour, to explore this little bundle of paper lovingly put together. We are proud to showcase our favorite pieces from the first year of our online magazine in a form that will allow the reader to take an entertaining break from the glare of the computer screen for just long enough to rejuvenate the senses and, hopefully, be inspired to write.

— Nicholas Litchfield

WAITING FOR THE TRAIN
Howard Waldman

Every minute I look around for possible witnesses. What would they think of an aging well-dressed clearly respectable man—that's how everybody has always seen me—acting like a thirteen-year-old up to no good, squatting next to rails in the middle of nowhere in mid-winter with night coming on, waiting with pennies for a train he'll never board? It's no crime but clearly abnormal. Isn't abnormality a crime in a way, though? That was always my father's view.

This time, driving back from the tire retread plant, I finally gave in to the abnormal idea about rails and pennies, and maybe more, that's been gnawing at me for the past month. I turned off the main road, something I'd never done before. It's a route so familiar from twenty-five years of back and forth from plant to home that it hardly registers anymore. I've covered plenty of ground in my life. Five eighty-mile round-trips a week, multiplied by 25 years, gives you 740,500 miles, twenty-nine times the circumference of the earth, a better trip than the real one, I imagine. Toward the end you'd probably get tired of equatorial temples and tigers too but not as fast as billboards and used-car lots.

So I turned off. The small road shook off landfills and junk heaps and started running in empty country alongside the railroad embankment. I pulled over and automatically pocketed the car keys. Halfway to the rails, I stopped. I went back to the Mercedes, left the keys on the driver's seat and then walked back to the embankment with a fistful of dull pennies.

★

I can't get rails and pennies out of my head ever since the doctor gently explained what's the matter with me. The gentleness was the really bad part. That was a month ago. Now I start thinking of rails whenever I see the faces around me, dull as unimproved pennies, the worst of the faces the one staring back at me in the bathroom mirror every morning. Maybe the illness has spread to my brain too.

Rails and pennies go back to when I was thirteen, already a secret sinner, standing at the bottom of the embankment, looking around for possible witnesses and then up at Allan. The wind blows his red hair into flames as he repositions the penny on the rail again. The penny is his idea. He has all the ideas and I go along with them, even the dangerous ones, because he's my only friend. I don't want to lose him. I've never told my parents about him because his father drinks, is an atheist, and has socialistic ideas or even worse. Everybody knows that in our small town.

Allan's up there without me not just because I don't dare soil my shiny Sunday shoes. Mainly because I'm scared of what that coin on the rail can lead to. I've heard that mutilating American currency is a Federal offence. Worse, suppose my father found out?

I think I can hear the train coming. I always liked trains. Before I studied geography, I used to dream about boarding one for China disguised as a Chinaman. But this train is different.

"Won't it derail?" I say, tense for flight and not mentioning the crime of mutilating Lincoln.

"So what?" he says and speaks about fat wallets scattered in the wreckage and what we'd be able to buy with the money. But he joins me as I start running away.

That evening the radio announces a train wreck: 200 victims. I'm devastated till I hear: India. Maybe kids there had been fooling around with rupees on the rails. My father tells mother and me to kneel with him and pray for the souls of those dead people. We do that all the time. There are lots of accidents and wars on the radio and my kneecaps hurt from them. But I always think of other things when I kneel alongside him, like being in China, for instance. This time I think about elephants and tigers in India.

The next day Allan and I recover the penny, miraculously transformed. Allan had placed it drab on the rail. Now after the train, it's unique, with a burnished true copper color, but green against the light, like, once, a sunset over our grey prairie town. It doesn't go round and round in a boring circle anymore. Lincoln's marvellously stretched out. I collect things like that. I have tropical seashells with the sound of those seas in them. I have cocoons with the hope of butterflies. I have old maps of spice islands in Asia. I have silk masks, lots of other things.

A kid at school offers us five drab round pennies for the marvel. I want to keep it. But Allan, already a shrewd schemer, is in command. It's just the start, he explains. Those five pennies, transformed by the train, will be good for twenty-five more pennies. Twenty-five multiplied by five amounts to 125. Three more such operations amount to 78,125 cents. He's quick at multiplication and sees the round money rolling in, 25% of it for me.

But we don't even get as far as the second operation. A railroad employee catches us recovering the five transformed pennies. He has silver hair, no lips and silver-framed glasses that magnify his pale blue eyes. Holding us by the scruff of the neck he says we deserve to be jailed for mutilating American currency and the name of God. He calls us Communists and kicks us hard in the behind, 78,125 times it seems. Of course he confiscates the transformed pennies. Then he takes our names. When I blubber mine he looks at me hard and says, "Hey, you're the minister's son." I should have denied it. But it's sinful to lie. I should have anyhow.

He reports us to our families. The next day Allan says his father just laughed. Allan's lucky. Not that my father ever beats me. He doesn't believe in physical violence, he always says. He confiscates. I learned the word from him very early. The last time it was all my Devil's Eye aggies and delicate bird skulls, because of cards on Sunday. This time he confiscates the tropical shells and the old maps and the cocoons and the masks. He also prays to God on my behalf. My soul's at stake, I understand. My mother weeps. I wish he'd beaten me.

That night I dream that Abraham Lincoln, terribly mutilated and wearing silver-framed glasses, sentences me to worse than jail. They are tying me to the rails in hell when I wake up sweating and weeping. I resolve to reform, be a good American, stop the secret sin, stop seeing Allan, respect my nation's currency and the name of God and never do anything that might turn me into a Communist.

My father died six years later. I was in business school by then, his idea, not mine. One day I poked around in his study, something I'd never dared to do when he was alive, and found in a deep drawer the aggies, the bird skulls, the cocoons (still just cocoons), the maps, the tropical seashells, the masks, and all the other confiscated things. They were dusty. I dumped them in the ashcan.

*

That business with the pennies was forty-six years ago. Since then I've been a reasonably good American. I've been married for thirty years, although it seems much longer, run my own tire-retread business in this same town, am a regular church-goer and try desperately to believe in transfiguration after death, contribute to charities, bowl on Friday evenings when my wife has her ladies' meeting, have sent three children through college and see them on Christmas most of the time.

I am generally regarded as dull but solid. Nobody knows how ill I am, not even my wife, although it's beginning to show. Probably it's like the main road with me: I'm so familiar to her I don't register any more. Nobody knows about that ill me, not at all solid. Nobody knows how I've been tempted to seek out rails in the open country as I've finally done and how I think of dull pennies transformed by the train's wheels into copies of rare sunsets over our town.

So here I am, midwinter, night falling, middle of nowhere, staring at rails, waiting with pennies for a train I'll never board. The way I did long ago, I look around for possible witnesses even though it's not for the same thing now. All I see in the twilight are muddy fields, bare trees, a grey sky and a distant farmhouse with lights already on at the end of the day.

I notice I've scuffed my new shoes struggling up the embankment. It doesn't matter this time.

I wish there were a way to retread souls like tires.

I think I can hear the train coming.

POINT NO POINT

Laury A. Egan

Did I visit this place once,
on an afternoon that skittered
between sun and rain?
I remember a desolate beach,
stepping on smooth eggs of stone,
past cedar logs lodged
like crowbars in the cove.
Did I photograph this scene then
or snap landscapes when asleep,
while walking in a dream?
In the scrapbooks stacked
against the wall, no pictures
of Point No Point exist.

Sometimes I wonder where it is,
this spot that defines futility.
Can we stick a pin in a map
and locate what might not be there?
Or, perhaps, despite seeing
where we wish to go,
we see no path; sometimes
we see a path but no destination.

On days when I feel lost,
on days when wind carries me off
to distant lands of restlessness,
on days like this, Point No Point
is where I am.

WALK OUT

Eric G. Müller

On hearing the news of J. D. Salinger's death, the memory of where and when I first read *The Catcher in the Rye* resurfaced with uncanny clarity—especially the circumstances that led up to that seminal read. It began with a haircut thirty-seven years ago.

As regards the length of hair, Damelin College was more tolerant than Bryanston High School, or all the public schools in South Africa, for that matter. The hair could cover the ears and the collar, but no longer. Of course, in emulation of the rock stars, I wanted it longer—much longer. There weren't many hair inspections, but when a teacher did walk round I stretched my neck as long as a giraffe's. When that didn't work anymore I curled my growing mane with my mother's curlers. That did the trick for a while. But I couldn't fool wily Mr. Le Roux, our hawk-eyed English teacher, for long. On one of his random checks he put his finger under a tight coil and slowly unfurled it until the naked, dark frond extended a full two inches beyond my white collar. As if he'd accidentally stumbled upon an exotic plant, he pulled out the rest of my carefully coiffed strands—one by one—and let them rest like hapless, succulent petals on my white collared shirt. "Now look'ee here," he said in a soft, sarcastic sing-song manner, "what an impressive display." Some students around me snickered. After a noxious silence he added, more severely, "See me in my office immediately after class."

I'd come to Damelin College to get away from exactly this kind of chicanery. I'd been 'caned' umpteen times at the other schools for having hair longer than the stipulated 'short back and sides' (and the breaking of other inane rules). As I reluctantly walked toward his office after class I was firmly resolved that if he caned me I would walk out of the school right there and then, no matter what the consequences. But what I got was even worse than a flogging. When I entered his office he already had a pair of scissors in his hand. Without a word he clutched a chunk of hair at the back of my head in his large fist and proceeded to cut it off straight above the collar, cursing when he realized how difficult it was—"Bloody thick hair!" Lock for licorice lock he threw my hair into the wastepaper basket. Once my hairdressing appointment was over, he said, "Don't you ever play that trick on me again, despicable youth!"

"And don't you ever touch my head or hair again—*sir!*" I yelled back, surprised at the vehemence of my impulsive retort. I rushed from his office, ran down the stairs and out into the busy city street. I took the first bus home, threw some food and a cooker into my backpack, and, fired along by the unabated momentum of my ire, hitchhiked out to the Magaliesburg Mountains, my place of primal refuge.

About five rides and three hours later, I was walking up the game trail to my favorite gorge when I was stopped by a baboon blocking my way. "Ah, Mr. Le Roux, here you are again," I thought, and eyed him out, unflinchingly. After a tense pause, the baboon turned and retreated back up the path. Relieved, I waited a few minutes before continuing. As I reached the top of the hill, I scanned the valley below and saw hundreds of baboons passing by, some with their young riding on their backs or hanging from below. He's multiplied, I thought, watching them in wonder. Once they'd dispersed, I hiked down to my favorite spot at Tonquani Gorge, where I rolled out my sleeping bag, made a fire, and began reading *The Catcher in the Rye.*

Though Holden's world was so foreign to mine, I couldn't help but note the similarities. His Pencey Prep school was my Damelin College, his Pennsylvania my Transvaal, his New York my Johannesburg, and his fourth school was my eighth. Like Holden, I had many grievances against the education system, and I was just as enmeshed in troubled relationships with girls as him. His sanatorium was my wilderness—my Tonquani Gorge. Instead of ducks, I had baboons. I read till it was dark, then made a fire, ate some sandwiches, brewed some Rooibos tea on my Cadac cooker, gazed at the stars and went to sleep.

Next morning I packed up and strolled back, reading all the while. Coming off the trail I stood beside the dirt road, waiting for a car. None came. I started to walk and read. I walked in the middle of the dusty road, with corn fields to my right— Holden's rye fields. Still no cars came and I continued walking and reading. An hour passed and a tractor that didn't stop. Mile after mile, page after page, on and on, alone on that windless road I walked. In between I broke off a *mielie* and tried to eat it, but the dried out corn was as hard as stone—cattle fodder. I continued my march and read, my steps falling into rhythm. It seemed odd to be reading about Manhattan, Central Park, taxi cabs and prostitutes, while I was trudging along this empty, red-earth road, corrugated by the cradled back and forth of rains and drought. I took off my white collared shirt and tied it around my head as a shield against the blazing sun, but tanning my torso. I walked and read to the sound of crickets and cicadas, the sonic equivalent of Holden's city drone. The two worlds of

Manhattan and the Magaliesburg merged steadily into one.

I was surprised when I saw the familiar bend in the road designating the end of the dirt road—I'd walked the twenty miles in a dream. And in a choreographed moment of uncanny coincidence I reached the Indian trading store just as I finished reading the last page of the book. I bought a pint of cold milk and a loaf of white bread and sat down in the shade of a dilapidated billboard (Three Trees Tea). Ten minutes later, still chewing and sipping my milk, I stepped up to the main road and within minutes hitched a ride back to Johannesburg, strangely pleased with myself.

And now, having remembered, I want to reread *The Catcher in the Rye* for a second time—to see how far I've come.

PHOTO CLUB PROJECT
Jennine Capó Crucet

The white lady follows me into the darkroom to see my pictures. I point to them as they hang from the string. I don't remember the right names she told me for the string and clips, but I show her the pictures anyway, hoping she'll see something more than what's there and tell me I'm a genius.

"This is my Tío Luis," I say.

She tilts her head to the side so that her eyes line up with the slanted paper. The white lady goes to the University of Miami, but she is from up north. She told me this the first time they came to our class looking for kids for the Photo Club Project—*up north.*

I see the picture, backwards, in her weird square glasses. I cannot tell from her mouth what she thinks of it. I shuffle to the next one and point.

"This one is of my dad. That's Tío Luis again, next to him."

In the picture, Papi is passed out next to his brother. Luis is half-watching the Marlins game on the TV. If you really look, you can see the TV's reflection in the window glass behind them and on the tipped-over beer bottles on the floor.

"Hmmm," the white girl says. I hope she asks me what time it is in the picture. She does.

"It's day time. Just after school. See out the window?"

She leans closer to the picture, tucks a piece of her feather-hair behind her ear. I love her hair because it's straight. Mine's very curly, but not so bad that it's pelo malo, like my brother's. Last meeting, she told me my hair was *luxurious*, that she wished she had it. I felt my face get hot and even reached up to let my hair out of the ponytail, but then I heard stupid Jorge, whose mentor is the black guy, whisper to Andrés next to him, Who, *her?* So I left it alone.

"Do they stay home from work to watch TV a lot?" she asks.

"Yup!" I say, too loud. My answer jumps around the room and sounds too happy. I look down at my flip-flops and step on my own toe. She puts her hand on my shoulder. When I look up, she tilts her head at me, and I worry about my heart now— that she can hear it beating.

Her hand falls from my shoulder as she moves to the next picture and laughs with her mouth closed.

"And who's this?" she says.

She very gently touches the back of the photo. Her glasses slip low on her nose, but instead of fixing them, she twitches her nostrils so that they crawl up on their own. She looks ugly when she does this, but I've learned by now that it means she's thinking. Then, for the first time today, I see her perfect white teeth. She's looking at the hands and feet in the picture, at the outstretched arm.

"That's my cousin Danny. He's doing the Soulja Boy dance. I know you can't see his face, but I still like it."

She had told the class that faces were the windows to the soul. Or eyes were—whatever. I felt bad when I developed the picture and saw that I'd taken it just as Danny had looked down, just before the Superman part of the dance. The Superman part might have made a better picture.

"This picture is excellent," she says.

"Really?" I say. Then "I thought so, actually."

22

She fake-frowns at me, but I know she likes my answer. She talks all the time about confidence. How confidence can save you, how it makes you better. How confidence gives you the power to do anything—even things you aren't good at.

"At what speed did you take this one?" she asks.

I freeze. I take all my pictures on the automatic setting because the camera belongs to the Photo Club Project and I can't break it. My mom had to sign a paper that said I was responsible for the equipment, and I when I told her what the English words said, I left out the part about having to pay for anything that got damaged. So I never touch nothing but the button that takes the picture.

"The regular one," I say, with extra confidence.

But it doesn't work, like she said it would. She puts her hands on her hips and stands back up straight. She looks down the string, at the rest of the pictures dangling from it, and says, "You don't know the speed at which you took any of these?"

I swallow hard and look straight at her eyes, at my eyes looking back at me in the blocks of her glasses. "I took them at the regular one," I say again.

"Sandra," she says, "The whole point was to experiment with film speed. That was the goal for this week. Why didn't you listen?"

I breathe through my nose hard, almost snort, like Papi does when I wake him up by accident taking a bottle out of his hand before it spills, or taking his glasses off. The white lady looks down and shakes her head, then whiffs past me. Pieces of her hair float away, trailing behind her as she leaves the dark room.

I look at the picture of Danny dancing. His feet are blurry. His fingers look like paws, with swirls the color of his skin linking them together, the top of his head a dark spot in the middle of the scene. Even though I use all my confidence, I

23

cannot figure out what makes the photo excellent. I decide to stay there, to stare at it until the blurs make something else, something better than just what I see.

BEAUTY
Phil Smith III

As soon as I saw the subject line on the email, I knew it was going to be one of those days. I really shouldn't complain. I have it pretty easy. I'm independently wealthy, and my job isn't that difficult, though it can be unpleasant when I have to turn folks down. Which I do, most of the time.

The message said that it was a woman, as usual, and that she'd be coming around ten. Since it was already 9:30, I figured I'd better shower and throw some clothes on, so I could at least look the part.

Sure enough, promptly at ten, the doorbell rang. I don't use servants—I'm not that lazy—so I trundled on downstairs and let her in.

"We're here to see Mr. Holder," said the man on the lady's right, whom I immediately knew had to be a lawyer. He confirmed it by offering me his card—So-and-So, J.D., Esquire, Partner, Dewey Cheatham and Howe, or some such. I vaguely recognized the firm's name, though not his.

"Good morning," I started. "I'm afraid that lawyers may not accompany—"

The woman cut me off. "But how am I supposed to be represented? And just who are you to tell me what I can and cannot do, anyway?"

They all make this mistake. Since they know I'm (a) rich

and (b) have ultimate power over their wants, they assume I should be tall and imposing. Instead, I look like the guy in the corner at the party who doesn't talk to anyone. Actually, I am that guy. Most of the time.

Anyway, it always goes like this, so I raised an eyebrow and introduced myself. "Thomas Benton Holder at your service, ma'am." I was pleased to see her blanch slightly at her gaffe.

"Oh. Um. Well. I guess …I guess you should wait in the car," she said to her companion, dismissing him with a wave of her hand and stepping forward slightly. I waved her in. As we proceeded to my office, she tried gamely to make small talk, complimenting me on my taste in decorating. I grunted a few times, but felt no great need to respond; this was closer to a trial than a business meeting, and as both judge and jury, I didn't need to make friends with her. In fact, I had a good body of experience that suggested that trying to do so would be a mistake.

"So, how does this work?" she asked, once we were seated in the den. "Do I explain why I'm here?"

"No, there's no need for that. I really just need to make my decision; there's no point in any argument."

"But …but …that's not fair! I was told that this was going to be a fair hearing!" she spluttered.

"Well, I don't know who told you that, but it will be objective. 'Fairness' is a relative term, and one I'm not prepared to debate at length; I'm sure you understand that." Actually, I was pretty sure she didn't understand that, but I wanted to avoid trying to explain it to her. She looked like she was used to getting her way, whether it was "fair" or not.

Sure enough, she started to protest, and then realized that doing so wasn't likely to endear her to me. Mercifully, that shut her up. And this alone showed me that, appearances to

26

the contrary, she wasn't as stupid and self-centered as my first assessment had suggested. I decided to try the rational approach.

"So, do you understand what's going to happen here today, and why?" I asked her. "Well, I understand that you're going to decide which group I belong in," she said, carefully. "I guess I don't really understand why you get to do that. Although," she added quickly, "I'm sure you'll do a fine job."

I love it when they try to flatter me. They don't realize that I honestly couldn't care less what they think. But she was trying, and I had time, so I decided I might as well explain it to her—not that it would make any difference if I had to refuse her petition later. "OK, let me give you the short version," I suggested, settling back in my chair. She nodded.

"Back at the turn of the century, air travel was popular and cheap. You may not remember those days." Actually, I knew darned well that she had been an adult well before the turn of the century, but it never hurts to let them think that you think they're younger than they are. She blushed slightly and nodded ambiguously, so I continued. "After 9/11, air security got tighter. And with every moronic 'terrorist plot', it got tighter still. After Richard Reid's 'shoe bomb', we had to take our shoes off. After the alleged 'liquid explosive' attempt, we couldn't take liquids on board. After the 'laptop bomb', computers were no longer allowed. Then there was the 'cell phone gun', and finally the last known terrorist attempt to date: the surgically embedded 'stomach bomb.' Of course, none of these actually worked. The stomach bomb might have, if the poor sap hadn't developed such bad abdominal pain before takeoff that the flight was held while he was removed on a stretcher.

"At the same time, the airlines seemed doomed, partly due to the market and partly due to their own stupidity. First, they eroded service bit by bit: no more meals, then they started charging for checked bags, then for on-board soda and snacks, then for pillows. Some of them even began auctioning off the good seats, and the right to board early—thus alienating their last allies, the frequent flyers, who were used to having these perks for themselves. About the only things they didn't get away with were pay toilets and charging for oxygen—although one airline did try the former briefly, until the FAA stepped in.

"The final straw came after the stomach bomb attempt. By then, we'd seen massive merger attempts, many of which failed, and several bankruptcies that stranded thousands of passengers. We were down to three 'real' airlines and a handful of regionals, all of whom were hemorrhaging money.

"And that's when good old Uncle Sam finally stepped in and nationalized the lot of 'em. This was good news and bad: the good news was that they weren't all going to stop flying suddenly one day; the bad was that we now had to pay realistic prices for airfares, with no discounts, no fare sales. Overnight, flying became the province of the wealthy and the business traveler, as it was in the early days.

"Besides the cost, the other thing that forced Ma and Pa to stop flying was the security crackdown. To avoid any possibility of on-board shenanigans, flyers who couldn't afford to pay several thousand dollars per year for permanent clearance now have to strip and undergo a CAT scan before boarding. And they can't take anything on the plane with them other than the electronic boarding passes issued at security.

"The fallout from this policy was a raft of complaints from 'beautiful' wealthy folks that they were being gawked at by 'ugly' people. While this griping was ignored at first, it garnered some serious attention when a Congressman was seen staring at Paris Hilton, with, um, obvious physical interest.

"And that's how you wind up here today: the Airline

Segregation Act of 2012 states that flyers shall be divided into 'beautiful' and 'other', shall go through security and board aircraft separately, and be segregated while on-board." I paused for effect.

"Yes," she finally interjected. "I was mistakenly classified as 'other', and have filed the forms and put up the bond to present my case to you today. I'm beautiful and should be classified as such! I—"

I held up my hand to stop her. "There's no point in arguing with me, ma'am. All you need to do is remove your clothing and I will make my decision. There's no need to be modest: this is my job. I have done so for almost a decade now, and have appraised hundreds of folks." Most of them women, I almost but not quite added.

She looked like she was going to argue anyway, then shrugged and stepped out of her dress. I have to admit, she wasn't totally nuts: twenty years earlier, she probably would have had a case. But time is unkind to the best of us, and it looked like she had also had several cosmetic procedures, some of which were less than successful. I told her she could dress.

"So?" she asked, anxiously.

I held up my hand and pressed the button that started recording.

"This is Thomas Benton Holder," I stated, adding my identification number, the date, and her case number. "I have examined the subject and the original ruling stands." I turned off the recorder.

"That's preposterous! I'll appeal!" She started to turn red; if it were possible, I think steam would have started coming out of her ears.

"I'm afraid there is no appeal. My ruling is final. That's it." I said it as gently as I could, although I knew it wouldn't make

29

much difference.

"But you never really answered my question before: why you? What qualifies you to be the ultimate judge of 'beauty'?" she asked.

"Simple," I replied. "In fact, you already know the answer. Think: what are my initials and last name?"

She thought a minute; no light dawned. Patiently, I explained: "Beauty is in the eye of T.B. Holder."

GOUT
Davide Trame

to Erri De Luca

A claw in the sinew,
an eagle's beak pecking
between bone and ligament.
And an eagle's eye reminding
in flashes of alertness
of how stone and bone come close
on the scree, under the sky;
how easily can a body
just drag itself, then crawl
and finally lie down,
becoming stone.

Nothing in the body
is made for soaring,
so, those who moved out
into the world of light
knew well
how to distrust the body
making another sinew grow,
like a butterfly breathing,
out of the claw.

AMERICA VERSUS MOUNT FUJI

Brinna Deavellar

A haiku:

Tokyo summer.
Humidity and concrete.
My face is melting.

In August of 2001, my two months in Japan were drawing to an end. This should have filled me with sorrow, but instead I found myself looking forward to returning to America, where I would no longer feel like the tallest woman with the largest feet in the history of the planet Earth. Sweat poured down my face in the sticky summer heat, as I thumbed through my guidebook in search of one final Japanese adventure. When my gaze fell on a photograph of the azure vista of Mount Fuji, my eyes widened. I had struck post-vacation-storytelling gold.

I peered over the book at my father. As a marathon runner, a lover of nature, and a vendor of fine life insurance policies, I knew that he was prepared for the challenge. "Dad, we should climb Mount Fuji before we leave."

He nodded, but a shadow of doubt flickered behind his eyes. He had only been in the country for one week, and so far not all of our tourist outings had gone well. Two days before, we had boarded the wrong train, ridden into the darkest heart of nowhere, and finally slunk back to the hotel after six wasted hours, depressed and broken. Despite our qualms, we nevertheless agreed to brave Fuji.

When we arrived at the bus station the following day, I expected to see a poorly-translated yet relatively straightforward sign reading something along the lines of, *Please for giving yen here and mounting bus there, enjoy your fun of Fuji climb.* Instead, we were greeted by a teeming crowd. Even though Mount Fuji is a popular destination for foreign tourists, signs written only in Japanese graced the walls. At a loss, we could only huddle at the back of the room. Eventually, we were given tickets by... someone, and dismissed with a vague wave to...somewhere.

By some miracle we managed to board the correct bus. While waiting to switch buses in the town of Kawaguchi, hours later, a crowd of schoolchildren swarmed around us and snapped photographs of our stunned faces, despite the fact that we had done nothing of interest except sit on a bench and look foreign. Confused and feeling like rare circus animals, we had no choice but to acquiesce. Thankfully, we were soon rescued by the arrival of the second bus.

The rattling monstrosity crawled through the villages at a pace usually reserved for severely impaired tortoises. I trembled as I imagined the engine exploding and sending shrapnel flying into our tender flesh. When we disembarked at the mountain's Fifth Station without any organ damage or signs of internal bleeding, I breathed a shaky sigh of relief.

Nothing compliments the awesome beauty of nature like a gift shop. When we stepped off the bus, our view of the mountain was thoughtfully blocked by a square building stuffed with postcards, walking sticks, and little drums from the movie *The Karate Kid, Part II*. Only through great force of will did we manage to resist the allure of such cultural treasures.

As we began our ascent, a voice cried out from the fog ahead. "Go back! Don't do it!"

We halted. A pale, trembling foreigner and his equally pale, trembling son stumbled down the hillside. The boy mauled a slice of watermelon while the father spun their tale of woe. "Everyone said the climb would be easy." He pointed to the fruit-eating boy. "He threw up halfway there and we had to get an oxygen tank..." His eyes widened as if wailing ghosts haunted his thoughts. "It's really bad. Don't do it."

Thanking them for the shining beacon of their optimism, we continued up the path. Ahead, the trees parted. A naked slope of muscle-grinding verticality loomed over us, its peak wreathed in clouds. Our delusions of rugged heroism evaporated.

"The guidebook says that children and grandparents 'regularly' make it to the top," I breathed, my head thrown back and my eyes trained on the spot where the summit might have been.

"Let's try it," my father managed, his face graying. "We're already here." Flanked by a crowd of foreigners and Japanese, we dug our boots into the earth. Dust and pumice rained down the path. For every step gained, a half step was lost as our toes slid backward on the sea of gravel. An hour passed. Familiar faces fell behind. When we reached ten thousand feet, thick mushroom gravy seemed to fill our lungs. My father waited in line at a way station to buy Hershey bars; he winced as he scanned the prices taped to the window. Stamping and shivering, we gobbled the squares of chocolate and slogged onward.

Time slowed with every step. "Only one hundred vertical meters to go," I gasped, my lips struggling to shape the sarcastic words in the thin air.

Cramps tormented our muscles as we wrestled with the

meager weight of the packs slung over our shoulders. When I summoned the presence of mind to raise my eyes from the ground, I realized that no one had crossed our path for some time. My face reddened as I imagined a crowd giggling at us from behind some camouflaged blind.

After an eternity, I glimpsed an arch spanning the path ahead. "We're here," I croaked, although given the dust in my throat the words probably sounded more like, "Warrgl hilr."

My father's only reply was a subdued grunt.

We milled over the barren moonscape that was the summit. The waning sun streamed into our eyes as we snapped photographs of desiccated rocks. While my father visited a pay toilet, I plucked one of the tourist guides from my pocket and scanned the departure schedule for the buses back to Tokyo. *3:30, 5:10, 6:20, and 8:00.* I glanced at my watch, cringed.

When my father shuffled over, I explained the treacherous bus schedule. "We only have a few hours before the last bus leaves Kawaguchi. If we get stuck there we'll miss our flight to New York tomorrow."

Once again, my father's only reply was a subdued grunt.

Our feet skated over pumice as we hurled ourselves down the path with reckless abandon. Snippets from my guidebook flashed through my mind: most tourists climbed Fuji to watch the sunrise. Therefore, there was no demand for evening buses back to Tokyo. We had picked the worst possible time to make the ascent. Now we risked missing our flight to the United States, a land of joy and wonder, where shoes and clothing glimpsed in shop windows might actually fit, and where most people have never heard of the fermented soybean nightmare that is *natto*. Soon, we spotted a fellow foreigner on the path ahead. "Is this the way to the Fifth Station?" he called. "I went the wrong way. I reached the top this afternoon, but I took the wrong trail and ended up climbing halfway down the wrong side of the mountain. I spent the last three hours backtracking."

The man's blunder alleviated our shame. We learned that his name was Mark, he was from California, and he was a runner like my father. I tuned out their conversation, for I sensed that a discussion of marathon times was imminent.

Darkness overtook us. As we retrieved our headlamps, we glimpsed movement on the path below. A Japanese teenager with no headlamp and clad only in a flimsy jacket struggled down the steep trail. Turning his head, he looked up at us with pleading eyes. We waved him toward us, and relief flooded his face as our headlamps pierced the deepening gloom.

The descent continued. When 7:05 PM crawled past, I was ready to hurl myself from the cliffs. That way, at least my corpse might reach the Fifth Station in time for the eight o'clock bus.

Finally, we stumbled back onto level ground. The Japanese youth thanked us and hurried into the night, perhaps unable to resist the siren song of the mugs and pencils at the gift shop.

My watch read 8:15 PM. Despite our heroic efforts, we had missed the last bus to Tokyo. Despondent, we hobbled aboard the shuttle bus bound for Kawaguchi. It was probably my imagination, but I could almost see the bus driver casting shaming looks back at us in the rear-view mirror.

When we arrived at Kawaguchi, I asked the bus driver for suggestions in halting Japanese. He replied that a taxi would come "soon." In the meantime, all we could do was wait. Mark had booked a room at a local hotel, but for the moment he was stranded just as we were. With mournful eyes, the three of us watched the empty bus career around a corner and vanish into the night.

Huddled in the dark, we waited. And waited. When I had finally resigned myself to spending the night on a bench, gravel crunched and two blinding lights swerved into the parking lot. I can only imagine the taxi driver's reaction when he saw three dirt-streaked foreigners frozen like deer in his vehicle's headlights. Most likely he heaved a grim sigh and dreamed of retirement.

My father waved money in his face while I asked in Japanese if it was enough for a ride to Tokyo. It was not, so he offered to take us to the nearest station where we could board a train bound for the capital. Mark, heart no doubt racing in panic at the thought of being abandoned in the gloomy night, asked if we could share a taxi. The driver shook his head and indicated that his hotel was in the opposite direction from the train station. I translated for Mark the driver's assurances that a second taxi would arrive to take Mark to the hotel after we had departed.

As we drove away, I glanced back. Clutching his pack to his chest, Mark watched our taxi vanish with wide eyes. For all I know he is still there to this day, waiting for a second taxi that will never come.

The driver raced through the night. At last, we arrived at the train station. My muscles shrieked in protest as I stumbled from the taxi. My normally gregarious father followed suit. He had not spoken for some time.

The taxi driver must have taken pity on us pathetic foreigners, for what happened next was one of our more amazing experiences with customer service. The man left the taxi, hauled our packs from the trunk, held them out so that we could shrug them onto our weary shoulders, led us into the train station, helped us purchase our tickets from the machine, and then inspected them to make sure that we had selected the correct destination.

Before the cynics scoff and attribute his kindness to greed for a larger tip, know that according to my guidebook, taxi drivers in Japan are not tipped. This point was eloquently demonstrated by the man's reaction when my father offered him all of our remaining money: two hundred yen, or about two dollars. At first I was embarrassed—if a taxi driver in America was given such a small tip for so much trouble, the tipper could expect to be, at the very least, disemboweled. Instead, this driver waved the money away with a smile. I could only gape as my father offered him the tip again, and then a third time, before the man acquiesced with a solemn bow.

The quest for Fuji was over. We boarded our flight on time the next day. When the airport personnel at JFK treated us like dirt upon our arrival, I knew that I was finally home.

In summary, climbing Mount Fuji is boring. Very boring. It is also difficult enough to hurt, but not difficult enough to brag about to one's relatives. But despite our disappointment, the most enduring memory of the journey for my father and me is that even though the trip was fraught with peril and setbacks, neither of us flew into a rage and tried to hurl the other from the cliffs. For my family, that is quite an accomplishment.

COMPASSION

Tim Conley

She had been the first to come home and found him, she told her husband half an hour later, when he too returned from a fairly depressing day of work, the kind of day when nothing goes wrong or badly, exactly, but there is a vague bite of disappointment with each passing hour. She had found the trussed man just as he was, right there on the front step. Was there a note, her husband asked, looking at the gagged man tied to the chair, trying to see past the bruises and burns and dirt to see someone he might identify. If there had been a note, she replied, I would have told you, I would have shown it to you, but as I have already said I found him just like this, no explanation. Her hands clapped together in front of her and held each other tightly, a habit she had assumed since quitting smoking in the winter, and she told him again that she had looked up and down the street of houses to see if anyone was about, pranking kids or someone who made a mistake, perhaps the wrong address, or even whether any of the other houses likewise had this sort of thing on their doorstep.

He's not a thing, her husband said sharply, but she answered, I don't know what he is, there must be a reason he's like this, beaten and tied up. They were both silent a moment, first wondering whether the bound man was conscious or not, because it was not immediately ascertainable though sure enough he was breathing, and next wondering whether they ought to take him inside. It was a sunny day, gradually eliminating the last small clumps of snow on various lawns and corners, and the three of them were fairly visible where they were. The husband asked his wife if he had been moved at all and, misunderstanding the question, she said that his head may have lolled when she went inside with the mail but she wasn't sure. I mean did you yourself move him at all, he said, and with a short glance that seemed to say, you should know better than to ask such a thing, she merely answered, I have been trying to think who we should call.

The husband set his coffee thermos and briefcase down on the cobblestone path to the house's front door and bent down to examine both the man and the chair to which he was tied. The latter looked to be of cherrywood, perhaps part of a very old office, actually the kind of quality furniture you don't see much of anymore, though its condition was nothing to boast about, for those scratches had really devalued the craftsmanship and it would take a lot of work to restore that chair, though, as the husband reflected, it would not be worse than the kind of pointless day of work he'd had at the office, in fact it would be much more meaningful, because after all of those hours of work you would have something to show for it, something solid that you could sit on. There was a smell of oil, at first he had thought it was furniture polish but of course that was just his fancy, this chair had not been near furniture polish for a good long time. Oil and also sweat, old sweat. One of the man's eyes was so swollen that it probably could not open and there was a long streak of purple down the opposite jawline. His hair had been very roughly cut but not washed for some time and his clothes, a much-torn, no longer white or perhaps beige shirt and what might have once been grey trousers, were filthy. Some of the stains were probably blood: his ribs were visible through a wide tear in the shirt and the sores there were raw. His bare ankles were deeply cut by the rounds of wire that strapped them to the legs of the chair.

Who should we call, his wife repeated, and her husband said, I'm thinking.

The wrists were firmly and repeatedly knotted behind with a thick and blackly stained rope, the kind of rope the husband supposed one would find in the rough hands of dockworkers and longshoremen, shoring up dinghies and the like. When he pointed this out to her, his wife wondered aloud what experience he had with such things, he had never been on a working dock in his life, she had never known him to swim, even. He knew she was thinking of a vacation at the lake the two of them had promised each other for a few successive summers, years ago, but always something had come up to prevent their going. He used to like swimming, really like it in fact, but that was before he had taken to wearing glasses, and now the thought of being underwater unable to see perfectly clearly made him uneasy in a way he could not readily articulate.

He said, I don't know, are you sure you don't know who he is, I mean have you taken a good look at him.

I don't want to take a good look at him, she answered, and now she was definitely thinking of a cigarette, but then she tried not to think of it because it had occurred to her when she had first arrived at the house and taken a good look at the bound man that the marks on his forearms could have been burns, burns made by cigarettes. Of course she had never before heard the sound of a cigarette being put out against flesh but suddenly thought she could hear it now, slowly repeating, a satisfying sound, a calming sound. She asked again who should be called, and suggested the police, but in a voice that let her husband know that it was not a strong suggestion.

Do you really want to do that, he asked without looking at her, now thinking about how difficult it would be to swim with one's hands tied, especially tied from behind.

We should at least bring him inside, his wife said, this time with more confidence, which she always had whenever her first suggestion was challenged or rejected, but she had no idea why she made this suggestion, unless it was out of worry that they must look extraordinary to anyone watching. Perhaps someone had already called the police, perhaps the authorities were already on their way, perhaps they should leave things as they found them.

They are calling for heavy rain, her husband surprised her by saying, by way of mild agreement. And they looked at each other for a moment, exchanging by weary marital telepathy concerns about how to lift the man and chair into the house and what difficulties might be involved, where in the house to place him, what to do with him after that, how long the rain might last, if indeed it were to fall. There were few clouds in the sky and none of them at all dark. The wife was about to remark on this fact when the sound of a siren made them both turn their heads, but it quickly faded away and they found themselves looking again at the man in the chair.

Why did you ask me if I knew him, the wife asked suddenly.

I thought you might, her husband shrugged, you know lots of people, I wondered if he was from around here.

Maybe I should ask you if you knew him, she said.

Know him, he corrected, not knew him, he's not dead yet, and why should I know him, I've never seen him before in my life.

Then why should I know him, she asked, why should I and not you, and don't give me that about my knowing lots

42

of people, at least the people I know don't come home to this sort of thing.

He's not a thing, he repeated with emotion.

Attracted by the rising volume of the conversation, the large-eared girl who lived down the street, known as someone whose curiosity often led her to being led home again by concerned adults, skipped into view and, when the husband and wife fell silent and stared at her, she advanced on them, brandishing a pair of safety scissors. She carefully looked at the man in the chair, then the couple, with many inscrutable blinks, and then gave her attention back to the scissors in her hand, whose action she demonstrated by cutting the air into strips.

Melissa, said the wife, unsure what else to say.

Scissor, scissor, scissor, came the reply, ess see eye ess ess oh ar.

When neither of them said anything for over a full minute, the girl became uncharacteristically bored and went skipping the way she had come. The husband had thought for sure that his wife would correct the girl, he was sure that she was fonder of children than she let on, and the wife was surprised that her husband had not told the girl that scissors was right and scissor was wrong, for she had little doubt that such errors grated on him. Both of them briefly wondered whether the girl had been testing them.

We should take him away from here, the husband said. He was again studying how hurt the man was and found himself trying to imagine what it would be like to punch a man like that, a man firmly tied to seat. It was hard not to imagine it once he had begun. He was not a violent man, had not thrown a punch since high school, but his imagination was generous now, entirely tactile in its offerings, so that his arm seemed to vibrate with the excitement, the pleasure of unprovoked fury, the revulsion.

That's a better idea, said his wife, than taking him into the house. There was no enthusiasm in her words, however. Both of them saw right away that there would be no way of getting him into either of their small cars, at least not without untying him from the chair, and the husband nearly said that if they had a pickup truck they would have no problem, they could just lift him up and put him, chair and all, just as he was, in the back, and though he did not say this his wife could tell even without looking at him that he was thinking exactly this, for he had long wanted a truck but she had not seen how it would be practical.

The phone rang inside the house and they both went in to get it. The wife was there first and said, Hello, and the husband stood near her, looking around the house, their house, the same as it had been when he had left for work that morning. Yes, they've been saying it's going to rain, but it hardly looks likely, she said, glancing at her husband, trying to read in his face what he was thinking as he looked around the house. He could tell from the voice she was using that it was neither her mother nor his on the phone but his concentration was elsewhere. His wife was saying that they sometimes get it wrong, who can predict the weather, while her husband was looking at the furniture and the carpets and the framed pictures and the appliances and thinking about how strange it is that none of them had changed, that they were all just as they had been when he had left for work that morning. That sounds very nice, but the thing is, no, I simply mean we can't this evening, his wife was saying, and he recognized that the voice she was using on the phone, a voice she used with certain friends and people from work, was strained but only strained enough that he would recognize it, not the person on the other end.

44

When she managed to say goodbye and hung up a few moments later, she found her husband sitting on the couch in the living room, lost in thought. She sat down in the armchair across from him, an old armchair they had both long ago agreed to replace, and waited for him to say something. There was no sound of rain outside. There was no sound at all.

He said, Let's have a child.

SUNLIGHT

Ron D'Alena

Fourteen-year old Danny Dunn ran headlong behind the Ford Model A pick-up truck. He ran barefoot, stretching out his left arm, trying to grab Roy's bouncing hand. As he ran, he could see Cooper Quill; laughing, one hand on the steering wheel, snatching glances over his right shoulder. Even Millicent, sitting in the truck bed next to Roy, was laughing. With a burst of speed, Danny sucked in his breath, seized the ridge of the tailgate, and hiked himself over and onto the wood plank truck bed.

Suddenly Danny remembered his mother. He twisted around and waved to her. She stood with folded arms at the edge of the dirt alleyway, in front of the white fence encircling their house. Hard working, his mother spent six days a week in downtown San Jose as a baker at The Staff Of Life. And never did she let the gossip over her being a divorcée wear her down. As Danny watched, she unfolded her arms, raised her hand and waved to him.

By and by, the four classmates reached the edge of town, where concrete road changed into graveled grade. This was Danny's favorite part of going to the swimming hole. He enjoyed the trees, boulders and meandering creek. Closing his eyes, he let the flicker of July sunlight through the tree branches dance against his eyelids. He felt as if he was swimming underwater, looking up at a surface agitated by some unseen disturbance. He imagined that imperfections in the surface water captured, carved up and erased the light. But always the light reappeared; it was never gone for very long.

Danny opened his eyes when Millicent tapped his elbow. The sunlight played with her chestnut hair and lit her freckled nose and cheeks.

Years later Danny wrote her a letter:

April 4, 1944

Dearest Millicent,

Last month in a small Italian village, thoroughly bombarded, I found a tin with one lemon drop. I pushed the tin to the bottom of my pack, intending to have the candy later.

We stayed in that village for three days. Then we moved on: working our way up the boot, walking to the point of collapse, stopping just before nightfall at an ungodly place crisscrossed with barbed wire and minefields.

Today we dug in. Beyond our trench, the forest is gone. There is only wasteland.

Behind us a road: pummeled every day by heavy artillery, traveled mostly at night during lighter bombing. We clean the road each morning: burying human pieces quickly, before maggots set in.

This morning an Italian woman came down the road. She carried a naked baby boy, bloody, half-dead. I gave the boy my lemon drop, and he smiled. The woman looked at me and said, Tomorrow come happiness.

Back in my trench her words seemed hollow, made

47

me weep. I want to believe there is truth in her words, but it's difficult after all I've seen, heard, and smelled.

It's raining again.

Please write me.

Yours Always,
Danny

The letter would go unanswered. And upon returning home, Danny would find Millicent—married to Cooper Quill, whose heart murmur had kept him from the war. But for now, there was only the beauty of sunlight licking Millicent's face and hair, and their closeness seemed everlasting to Danny Dunn.

LOLA
Lisa Abellera

I know you through the rich dark brown soil
crumbling in my fingers like chocolate cake.
I imagine your nurtured bell-shaped papayas,
coaxing their smooth, leathery skin
from green to yellow,
while mangoes, the colors of the island sunset,
hung with their tantalizing sweet scent,
as you tended to them as only a mother could.

I have seen you only once,
in a weary black and white photograph
creased with years of reverent storage
in your son's weathered leather wallet.
Bamboo trees stretching their slender tips
and banana trees fanning their thick leaves
in the tropical breeze
while you sit surrounded by your boys
in your rattan chair
that cradles you like a queen.

His homage to you remains
in those sour green apple,
thick bumpy-skinned lemon

and fuzzy orange apricot trees
that grew up with me.
Like you, he returned
to the earth, the same earth
that feels my sun-browned calloused hands
as they coax these speckled pears
from green to yellow,
while thin-skinned Meyer lemons
hang like Christmas ornaments
and oranges the size of softballs
offer up their warm, sticky sweet nectar
as if to raise a glass to you.

MAY PROSTITUTES ONLY TAKE CASH
Tyke Johnson

I can no longer go shopping. I own enough suits, jackets, slacks and shoes I'll never wear. I can no longer go to malls, can no longer get my haircut. I own enough hairspray and hand cream. My nails look just fine. My hair will never be unhealthy again. I didn't need any of it. I didn't want any of it. But I bought it and own it and will buy it all over again unless I just stay home forever.

There are too many things for sale, too many sales people, too many men with cool clothes and stylish hair. Too many foreign women with caressing touches and rolling tongues—each willing to stand too close and look into your eyes, never blinking, telling you how nice your cuticles *could* be.

They see me trying to look away. I'm looking for an exit but the shoes that they've taken from the back of the store are right there and they really want me to buy them. They've worked so hard after all. They've done exactly what their job was, nothing more. Their service wasn't all that great but that doesn't mean they shouldn't be rewarded, right?

So I buy them. They barely fit but screw it, they're right there, right now, in the box waiting and the salesman is on his knees lacing up the left shoe to make sure I like that one as well. Unbeknownst to him, I don't like the right shoe. There's little chance of me liking the left. He doesn't know this, of course, because I've not said so. I've only nodded and agreed with him when he pointed out that *one-ten isn't all that much for a shoe like this.*

He's right. One hundred and ten dollars isn't all that much for a pair of shoes I have no need for. A pair of shoes that doesn't fit all that well and can only be worn with about four percent of my clothes—though I'm going to Macys after this. Who's to say they won't have some outfits that match these shoes perfectly? And that's just it; they will or they won't, but I'll buy them anyway because a salesperson just like him will tell me to.

I'm not rich. In fact I have little disposable income, but credit cards were created with people like me in mind. Some genius psychologist realized one day while shopping with his awkward son for corduroys that his son was the ultimate spender because he couldn't say the simplest word—no. He just didn't have the capacity to break the hearts of so many sales people by telling them those *corduroys are too tight and too blue.*

Seeing this, and assuming there are probably thousands out there just like his son, who simply needed the financial means to say yes to everything, the entrepreneurial analyst created plastic money.

It's worked miraculously for I was able to buy that suit from Celio, which the salesman, in all his courtesy, couldn't have hemmed for me in three days time. Never mind that the pants were too long. Never mind that I was the only customer in the store—something I now avoid entirely—and was spending six hundred dollars. Never mind I had to fly Paris and take a train to Bordeaux, to buy the unnecessary suit in the first place. And now, because of that ingenious credit card creator, I can buy these too-pointy leather boots at my feet.

I find solace that *this* salesman, the *one-ten isn't all that much* salesman is at least refraining from pitching the suede cleaner or leather protector or shoelace sanitizer. He seems to be a merciful god and is letting me off with just the ill-fitting boots, which look terrible with the jeans I wear a majority of the time—a point he chooses to ignore.

It all started in Palm Harbor, Florida where I spent the latter two years of high school. After having worked for a couple months at Target I decided it was time to treat myself to a few things. First of those things was a new pair of sneakers. On my day off I drove to the mall and went in Foot Locker.

Growing up, all shoe shopping was done at large warehouse sports stores—the ones with common first names such as Bob's in Milford, Connecticut—whose collection of sneakers were a year or more old. This was my grand opportunity to shop where all my friends from childhood were able to shop. Where everyone else bought their basketball shoes, their Nike Airs and Reebok Pumps, while I strutted around in LA Gears and British Knights.

I entered Foot Locker with a full head of steam, of freedom and opportunity, but quickly became disconcerted by how expensive the shoes really were. I was making $5.50 an hour and each shoe I was interested in cost a weeks' wage. And though I enjoyed working with Joe, the fat, gay cashier addicted to pills with bleached hair who offered to give me a blow job in the bathroom before I went in for my first interview, I wasn't sure spending it all on shoes was worth it. But as I was about to leave, as I was whispering apologies to my dad for complaining about being forced to choose from the lower racks, from the racks near the back, the racks without a display, I was slapped from behind on the shoulder. And the blow, though slight at best, woke me from my daydream of guilt.

He was a blonde guy about my height at the time, probably

5'9", and wearing the referee uniform of Foot Locker. He wore an earring and several rings, all silver, which didn't seem to set his confidence back any and though a puka shell necklace was tight against his active Adam's apple, he spoke without impedance.

"What can I help you with, Chief?" We were off to good start. He had already referred to me as dominant figure of a mostly extinct people. "What's your name?"

"Tyke."

"Tyke? Cool name dude. I'm Hunter. So whaddya do, Tyke?"

From there rolled the standard round of salesman questions to make a potential buyer open their door so he can casually send in, as if by messenger pigeon, the idea that whatever it was he had, would certainly improve upon anything I had.

His girlfriend used to go to East Lake High School just like me. "You just missed her, Man. She graduated in '93."

Not willing break down the validity of his use of the term "just," it was 1997 after all; I gave in to his best friend, big brother demeanor. "That's awesome."

He continued his barrage of just-about-there commonalities.

"And by the way, Dude, don't tell anybody this, but I stole an Xbox game from your Target a couple months back." He laughed and nudged my shoulder as if confiding in me the fact that he also sucked on Karin's breasts in the woods on our eighth grade field trip. "But hey, let bygones be bygones right?"

"Ha, no I won't say anything," I politely joked back.

"Awesome, Man. It's all good, right?"

"Oh yah. Totally. Definitely all good." As the words were coming out of my mouth I could feel something happening to me. I could feel myself losing all control of my actions, both words and movement. I was losing control of my feet as they walked towards the "basketball" section, losing control of my eyes as I scanned the sea of shiny patent leather high tops. I couldn't have wanted a pair of shoes less but there I was getting right in there for a close up. I was picking up, handling, a pair of And 1 brand shoes. As far as I knew they only made t-shirts with faceless mannequin like figures whom, also wearing And 1 gear, were dunking or shooting or, most importantly, talking trash. The only player I knew who'd even had their shoes was Xavier McDaniel whom I despised since he played for the New York Knicks.

"You like them? They're pretty sweet shoes. I've got a pair just like 'em. Use 'em when I play ball over at Countryside."

Before I could even respond, before I could remember how much I truly hated Xavier McDaniel, how treasonous this purchase would be to my Bulls, I was nodding and agreeing. "They're pretty damn comfortable."

Soon after I was agreeing that about *ninety-five dollars, after taxes*, wasn't all that much to spend on a good pair of basketball shoes. Never mind the fact I had come in to purchase a casual pair of low tops so I could have a little confidence to meet new people at my new school. Goliath style footwear with a zipper and a stitched man dunking on the ankle didn't seem the most conspicuous way of introducing myself at still foreign lunch tables. There were only so many more days I could handle hearing the two freshman's obnoxious laughter that were my tablemates.

"You wear a size ten too? That's awesome, so do I," he said coming back from the secret recesses of the Foot Locker back room. He kneeled in front of me and laced up the right shoe for me. I stared and wondered how I was going to pay for these bastards of footwear. I only had sixty dollars, leaving me about eleven hours of work short, after taxes.

As all the misfortune of the broken mirrors would have it, they fit astoundingly well. His thumb, pressing against the end of my big toe, proved this. "What more could a guy ask for?"

At that moment, I didn't have any idea how to answer that question. There was very little, if anything, a guy could ask for in the world besides fitting footwear.

After Hunter had them wrapped back up in the box and in bag on the check out counter he grabbed a white spray bottle from beside the register.

"You know what this is?" Hunter asked as if a spray bottle was oft confused with a billion dollar NASA tool and not something a toddler could master. "It's leather protector," he continued before I had a chance to say anything. "Check it out."

He grabbed what I assumed was the designated "test shoe," also known as the unassuming low top I had hoped to purchase. He sprayed it a couple times and looked up at me.

"Just spray and you're done."

"Done with what?" My pride in finally speaking up showed too wide in my eyes and breath and he took back the lost ground immediately.

"Done with cleaning your shoes. Done with buying a new pair every four months because the leather's ruined. Spray the shoe once over, every six months or so, and guess what?" As if I had any intention of speaking up again. "Your shoes will last forever. It's really an amazing thing. You don't have scrub or anything. Just spray 'em and you're out the door."

"Cool." I had unknowingly chosen to speak monosyllabically from that point on.

"For sure. And its super cheap for what it does. Only seven bucks and you've just saved yourself a hundred or more dollars in replacement shoes. You know?"

"Nice."

So you want me to add that to the order.

"Sure."

Not to leave any men standing on the battlefield he casually mentioned how socks were on sale. Could he ring me up a pack? "Three for a measly twelve bucks. And they've great support for your game." Presumably my basketball game, which I guess I was going to resurrect in the upcoming tryouts. I hadn't any intention of it. Then again, perhaps it was just because I didn't have a new pair of basketball shoes.

"Great."

Hunter smiled big, happy to have helped me spend twice as much as I had planned. Smiled that is, until I opened my wallet and admitted I only had sixty bucks. But my escape was not meant to be. Hunter knew the lay of land too well. He'd been raised in these jungles. He could navigate the canopy rivers blind folded.

"Ah, Tyke don't worry bout that. You can just charge it." He pointed at, almost touched, a teal MasterCard next to my license. If I took another second to react I believe he would've simply taken the card out himself and finished the transaction without me—sign my name and all.

"Oh." I had never used the card before. I only had it for emergencies. You know, in case I was driving in the Everglades and lost a tire and I had to pay a tow truck to get me out of there before the alligators could feast on another stalled motorist.

"We take MasterCard," Hunter, ever the gentleman, informed me.

"Good."

And that was it. Moments later I was signing my name to my first charged item in my life and moments after that I was leaving Foot Locker with a pair of shoes I never wore once.

Upon leaving I took a seat near a large fake plant in a giant terracotta pot. Next to it was a kiosk selling baseball caps. A young guy with brown spiky hair looked over at me. I must have looked terrified. I must have looked like I lost my house in a game of poker, lost my child to the black market, because my opponent had pocket cowboys.

"Can I help you with anything?" he asked, ball cap in hand.

I looked up wide eyed and out of breath, then fled without answering, nearly forgetting the shoes, and ran all the way to my white Chevy Corsica. When I got inside I wondered how my dad was able to purchase such a mediocre car eight years prior. Not an automatic thing on it. And aside from realizing that I was a weak and pathetic boy, I also realized my dad was a true man. He didn't want to spend a week's wage on heated seats and headlight wipers, on the newest and coolest shoes for my three brothers and I. After all, he still had to buy the gas.

I threw the bag into the backseat and drove off in disgust, vowing to never set foot in a mall again.

That was ten years ago and I've broken that promise time and time again, and time and time again I've spent money on things I didn't actually want. I'm breaking that promise right this very second.

I have theories as to why I'm like this. The first is founded in guilt. It's based on the fact that these people, these sales people, are just trying to make that money, just trying to pay those bills. When they speak to me, I'm hardly paying any attention because I create whole worlds for them, which always include dire financial straits. A world in which the money they'll make on my purchases' commission will be able to pay the electric bill, will allow them to warm their houses for one more desperate week. This is also why when I'm asked upon checking out *if anyone helped me* I always point someone out even if by some miracle no one actually spoke to me.

Another theory is that I have a subconscious desire for everyone to like me, even complete strangers whose only interaction is script and rhetoric. This causes me to do any number of unnecessary and probably equally unnoticeable actions. When I'm in any store, even those that sell items obscenely out of my price range, I'll still look at things as if I might purchase them. There might not be a soul around, but not to seem poor, to seem undesirable, I'll look a sport coat over, casually regarding the price tag and audibly saying things like *not bad* while acting as if I'm even at all considering its purchase.

How this acting looks I can only guess. I don't have access to any of the closed circuit cameras but I believe it usually involves: feeling the fabric, lifting the arms, checking the cuff links, smoothing the inside of the collar, and saying, *nice* over and over.

In my head I want these people to see me as someone capable of buying such an item but even though I seem to be infatuated with it, I don't. Presumably, I'm interrupted by a phone call and have to leave the store when in actuality I'm talking to an inanimate electronic.

The danger, of course, is that with such fake interest I risk the chance of a salesperson coming up and speaking to me, which leaves me further in debt than I was moments prior when I didn't feel the need to buy a velveteen suit or cashmere scarf i.e. the Celio scene mentioned above.

When I get home I put the *only one-ten* pointy boots in a closet that's already full of boots, already full of filling hangers. I go to the bathroom and see that the drawer is full of hair products and hand products, sprays and shines, butters and bath salts, never used and never thrown out. I've shaved my head to avoid the uber hip barbershops with their boutique products. I've sewed pockets and safety pinned shirts and shorts to avoid department stores with their endless swarm of complimentary women. Closing the drawer I pray I never come across an equally complimentary prostitute and if so, may she only accept cash. I'm tired of making that scheming psychologist so rich.

THE SHOOTING PARTY

Jack Frey

The town was just a long curve of hotels and nightclubs on the Gulf of Siam. Sandwiched between the tourist spots and the smouldering wall of trees beyond was a second curve of corrugated shacks and thatched huts, where the regular folk lived.

Truth be told, I felt more at home among the huts than the hotels. For two years, I'd been working with rural farmers in the northeast to improve vegetable production. I was happy enough to stay in the village year-round, but I had been obligated to come to the city for a conference. The meetings were over for the day, and I was now on my own.

I stood in the hotel lobby, my back pressed against a tiled pillar. It was Saturday night, and the thudding pelvic beats of the disco on sixth floor were making the hotel shiver. I watched the endless coming and going of men with wide collars and bare chests and gold jewellery, women with high boots and miniskirts. Twice already, I'd politely declined the offer for "a private party". These places made me uncomfortable. I left the hotel.

Streetlights pierced the sidewalk here and there, bronzing rivers of silt that trickled towards the beach. Below the road, closer to the water, was a restaurant of bamboo and thatch, strung up with coloured lights and studded with a Boy Scout's sash of round metal beer logos.

There were people milling beneath the sherbet-hued lights. A slight breeze carried the smell of smoke and char-grilled fish over the wet sand. I listened. There was no thumping dance music, just the quiet murmur of voices, so I went closer.

As I approached, a woman moved to the top of the steps leading to the tables. I guessed that she was in her sixties—hard to tell in that light—and probably European, dressed in a light sarong and cotton top. She eyed me as I crossed to the bar and ordered a drink. Pineapple juice with just enough vodka to make it worth the five bucks I'd pay for it.

The woman came up alongside. Her face was flushed, as though she'd already had a drink or two. She smiled in an awkward way that made me nervous.

"Excuse me," she said. "I wonder if you might be—"

I waited for her to finish. But when she said nothing, just looked at me with nervous and expectant eyes, I shook my head and sipped hard on my pineapple juice. I hoped that when I took my eyes out of my glass, she'd be gone.

"Probably not," I said.

She frowned, wobbled a little. I think she was contemplating whether or not to retreat. But instead she wiped her hands on her sarong and said, "Well, in that case, I guess I was stood up."

"Sorry to hear that," I said, and drained the glass. You've got to understand, I didn't mean to be an ass, but the woman was at least thirty-five years my senior. I set the glass on the bar with a few bills and made for the stairs.

The woman followed me, first with her feet and then with her eyes as I moved across the sand. Fifty paces later I stopped, turned to look. She was standing at the railing, lonely eyes still on me.

"What's your name?" I asked, feeling a little guilty. My voice was flat against the rolling surf.

"Hilda," she said.

Then I had visions of my grandma standing there, all alone since my granddad passed away, and I softened. As long as she kept it friendly, didn't try anything gross, she could tag along. "I'm gonna take a walk," I said. "Care to join?"

Hilda smiled again. She tiptoed a little unsteadily across the sand and took my arm.

"I'm Dutch," she said.

I nodded. Waves tumbled on the glassy strip at the water's edge, stirring up the algae, making it glow speckled-green. Palm fronds hissed in the breeze. The moon was sliding up over the sea, filmy behind the clouds, chipped and gnawed like a waxy jawbreaker.

Hilda told me then about her weaving consortium, International Hands. It was based in Rotterdam, with offices on every continent. Hilda was struggling to record the disappearing art of local basket weaving.

"What do you do, dear?" she asked. She patted my arm.

"I work with vegetable farmers," I said.

Hilda smiled again. "That's nice, dear." She rested her head on my shoulder.

The beach narrowed to a point where the street was only a dozen yards off. A streetlight burned, yellow light catching on shards of broken glass embedded in a wall that followed the sidewalk. Beyond it, an ancient villa crumbled like graham crackers in the tropical night.

A gate split the wall, two panels of corrugated tin. A man called to us from the gate, an American by the sound of it. He wore slacks and a loose-fitting collared shirt, kromah knotted around his neck.

"Hey, over here," he said. "Got a real party going on inside."

Hilda led the way, across the street and through the gate, to a courtyard where a row of stunted papaya trees hugged one wall. From the villa I heard music, trickling through slats high in the wall and pouring over the veranda. It was mellow, the sort of saccharine jazz that twists my nerves, makes my teeth ache. One of those parties, I thought.

At the side of the house was a fleet of cars—everything from Toyota Corolla to Land Rover to Mercedes-Benz. A cluster of men hung beneath the awning, local drivers, the embers of their cigarettes pulsing in the darkness.

Hilda was speaking with a couple on the steps, a man and a woman, both of them horrifically tanned. Their skin resembled smoked sausage. They spoke together in French, a language I can sometimes understand if the conversation topic is right. On this occasion, I understood nothing.

At length, Hilda turned to me, excited. "There's a famous American actress inside," she said. "Eva Daggert."

Even I, a total dunce cap when it comes to pop culture, knew of her. The only movie I'd seen with Eva Daggert—the name of which I couldn't remember—she played a woman on the run from the CIA. She'd witnessed some crime, or committed it maybe. Either way, the movie ended with her balanced on the lip of a dam in Kazakhstan, clothing soaked to her curvy body, helicopters hovering overhead. At least that's what I remember. She'd gotten a big name lately for the work she'd been doing in along the Gulf. Mobile reading rooms for kids, or something like it. There was talk about a Nobel Peace Prize.

Inside the villa it could have been anywhere—Hanoi, Casablanca, Paris. Paris in August maybe. Hanoi for sure. Strips of track lighting dangled from the ceiling like bats, illuminating the Warholian prints that clung to the yellow walls. There was a bar at one end of a vaulted room, and a kid in white laid out drinks with apparent apathy. I thought about some of the farmers I worked with. They had never been to a place like this. I suddenly wanted nothing more than to be back in the village.

So far I had avoided looking at people. But I looked now. They were clumped along the fringes of the room, leaning on chairs, sipping on drinks. I thought I could label them on sight—the Aussies, their sunburned chests gleaming like polished leather—the Dutch oil experts, in from the platforms on the Gulf—the Canadians, desperate not to be mistaken for Americans. Some were laughing, others were nodding in that serious way people do when they've had a few. The music was loud, and they leaned in close to hear one another.

"Can I get us a drink, dear?" said Hilda, putting her lips close to my ear. I felt her fingertips move along the curve of my spine.

"No, thanks," I said, flinching.

A young boy slipped past my elbow, balancing a tray of drinks. Hilda took up a tall sleeve of champagne and put it to her lips. She tilted it back, and just as the last sip disappeared into her mouth, she winked at me. Then she stumbled towards me, wrinkly old hands grabbing for my shirt, and every nerve in my body, every tendon, was tight. I was a mousetrap, ready to snap, ready to make a dash for the door.

But I didn't have to run. Before my eyes, Hilda's face morphed from an aging caricature of seduction to one of total enthrallment. She tugged my sleeve, then pointed over my shoulder. She was gesturing in the direction of a massive stone head, something that belonged in the National Museum, not here. But Hilda wasn't looking at the statue.

"There she is," she said, hissing point-blank into my ear. "Eva."

And so she was, standing beside the head with her back to us. She was dressed for the Oscars, and I suddenly felt unforgivably shabby, as if I were wearing nothing but a fur loincloth.

We stepped closer. I felt myself melting in the heat of the woman's presence. I wasn't fighting it anymore. I couldn't. There was something electric about her, about her back that gleamed beneath the track lighting like the hood of a sleek, bronze sports car. We were close—so close I could have reached out and touched her, could have shammied her hood.

The music was quiet now. It had devolved into what I believe is called *ambience*, but could have been the soundtrack to a journey into the black depths of the Mariana Trench. The music was quiet enough for us to hear the conversation that surrounded Ms. Daggert.

"That's wonderful," said a woman, lips glistening. "So wonderful."

"Well," said Eva, "if we don't work together for a solution, then the children will suffer."

A man spoke up, a man whose throat looked as though it had been speckled with corned beef. "Ms. Daggert, I understand that you've also been working with a project concerning laptops. Could you share a few words?"

Eva paused. "Our hope is to bring about technological convergence. To level the playing field, so to speak. A laptop for every child."

The little nucleus of people about her sighed, and she continued. "Every child should have access to the internet, wherever they live, so that they can communicate with other children around the world. Imagine! A girl living right here could talk with a girl in Seattle or London. They could share their hopes and dreams, their fears—"

At that point, I audibly scoffed. I couldn't help it. Maybe I should say that my body scoffed as an auto-response, the way a person will shut their eyes when a bee flies at their face. I scoffed, loud enough for everyone to hear. The circle went silent.

Ms. Daggert turned to face me. I don't think she was used to being scoffed at, because her expression was almost curious. "Something wrong?" she asked.

I shook my head. "No."

"But you scoffed."

"Did I?"

"Yes, I'm sure you did."

"Just a bit of phlegm in my throat, I guess," I said. "Dusty in here."

"You scoffed," said Eva.

Hilda was staring at me with fear in her eyes. I shrugged. What the hell, I thought. "Alright, I scoffed. So what?"

"I'd like to know why."

I thought a moment. "Ms. Daggert, I work in this country. It might surprise you to learn that most people here don't have track lighting or Pop Art or open bars. They don't have drivers waiting for them outside." I waved my arm towards the stereo system. "They don't have these kind of luxuries. Might not even know that they exist. You know what I mean?"

Eva stared at me with her mouth open. The others looked ready to lynch me.

"Listen," I said. "It's just that half the kids you're talking about don't get enough to eat. Laptops aren't much good out here."

A freckly woman beside Hilda spoke out. "How can you say that? You're just trying to keep those kids out of the twenty-first century. You're nothing but a neo-colonialist."

I sighed. "Lady, where I live, there are no power lines, let alone internet access. Jeez, I don't even have running water. And you want those kids to hop into a chatroom with Sammy from Duluth?"

I felt as though I'd just stomped on a nest of rotten goose eggs. The air was thick.

"What about solar power?" suggested Corned Beef.

No one said anything. Eva's skin had a ruddy glow to it that I realized was probably anger or embarrassment, or both. I wished the lights would just go out.

And they did. At that moment the music and the lights both died. A power outage, as common in those parts as starfish at low tide. For half a second, no one made a sound. We were parrots with blankets over our cages.

From somewhere at the back of the villa, a loud growl started up, the generator roaring to life. Then the lights came on, blinding us. No music this time.

Ms. Daggert was staring at me, ready to say something, but she didn't have the chance. Just as her lips began to move, the air shattered into a thousand pieces. World War III, or the closest thing to it. Machine gun fire, very close. In real-life it never sounds the way it does in the movies, rich and chocolaty and masculine. This was the real McCoy, high-pitched and hollow, like strings of firecrackers in a tin can.

Someone screamed, and the kid with the champagne dropped to the ground with a splash and a spray of glass. Corned Beef jumped on Eva—probably spent the rest of his life dreaming about it—and pressed her to the floor. Me, I took Hilda.

We laid there for what felt like hours, the rattle and pop of automatic weapons creating a new sort of ambient noise. Hilda took the opportunity to get a few unwanted squeezes in, until I finally clamped her hands to her sides. We waited. The sounds

68

didn't come any closer, and I felt my pulse slowing.

It was only later that we learned about the rich Singaporean who owned the villa next door, about how he took special joy in collecting firearms from across the world. And just as the little party for Ms. Daggert was losing steam, his troupe of visiting Russian investors was really getting into the scotch. It seems that they persuaded Mr. Chen to open one of his gun cases, the contents of which they took to the roof in an attempt to shoot down the moon.

I ended up apologizing to Eva. I said I hadn't meant to make her look like an idiot. And I definitely wanted what was 'best for the kids'. It's just that people need to eat. And you can't eat laptops. Not without a lot of salt.

BUTTS-UP

Tom Mahony

The friendly game of butts-up took a dangerous turn when the case of Pabst Blue Ribbon arrived. The game involved throwing a tennis ball against a wall and catching it on the rebound. If you dropped it, and didn't touch the wall fast enough, you had to stick your ass in the air while other players nailed you with the ball.

As Smitty, Joey, and I drank the beers, our agility suffered. Oafish Smitty was the first to flounder. Joey and I pelted him without mercy. The beers lowered our accuracy but increased our velocity and curious thirst for vengeance. The resulting carnage was disturbingly addictive.

"Does this game seem weird to you?" Joey said after a throw.

"Yeah," I said. "A little."

But it wasn't time for introspection. It was time for pain and humiliation and avoidance thereof.

As I prepared to pummel Smitty yet again, my wife approached.

"Dinner's ready." She paused and glanced around. "What are you guys doing?"

"Nothing," I said.

She nodded toward Smitty, still on the ground with his ass in the air. "What's he doing down there?"

I lowered the ball and grudgingly explained the game.

"That's so pathetic," she said.

Joey and I shrugged. Smitty mumbled something but, hunched over, it looked like he was talking out of his buttcrack.

She just shook her head and walked away.

Joey muttered an apology and headed for the house. My adrenaline evaporated and I suddenly felt stupid. We were pushing forty, guzzling lukewarm PBR, and hurling tennis balls at the upturned ass of a grown man rather than talking art, finance, and politics with the real adults back at the dinner party.

Pathetic, indeed.

I started toward the house, but something pulled at me. Some primal force acquired on the childhood playground and never fully abandoned, unlike the immortality that faded long ago.

I turned and hurled the ball and as I heard the flat dull thud of impact and Smitty's howls of pain I couldn't help but smile.

Nailed him.

STEVIE AND LOUIE

Michael Connor

I was young, and a tourist, and in Austin, so I was on Sixth Street. Also, I was drunk. I found Sixth Street similar to South Street in my hometown, Philadelphia. There are the out-of-towners steered there by a tip from a website or concierge. There are the college students with fake I.D.s. There are the cops on bikes. There are the bars: the hipster dives, the jock spots, the douchebars for douchebags. There are the t-shirt shops and general bric-a-brac vendors vending general bric-a-brac. I was aiming to get drunker and listen to some live music as I pulled out my camera and snapped a picture of a big brown building that looked just fancy enough to be historic.

"You havin' a good time?" came a voice from behind me. I turned to see a crustache across a broad, yellow grin. The crustache wore a cap advertising Miller Lite and wielded a Big Gulp cup. Back in Philly, my reaction to this figure may have been something along the lines of "Face, muthafucka! Get out of mine!" However, as I mentioned, I was a young, drunk tourist, and felt like maybe this simple Texas sketchball wouldn't lead me into a dark alley where I'd be beaten, robbed, and sodomized. So I responded in a more affable vein.

"Oh yeah. Great time."

"Visiting Austin? I noticed the camera," he said, sucking at the straw of his Big Gulp. I had only been in town for two days, but already noticed that if I snapped a picture, people would ask me where I was from. This was all very eye-opening for an East Coaster. If I see someone snapping a picture back home, I don't get the urge to play good host. I just consider the fact that their rental car is making it harder to find parking in Center City.

"Where are you from?"

"I'm from Philadelphia," I told him. "Heard Sixth Street is the place to be for some nightlife."

"This is a party street," he said. "You should be here on the weekends. The cops block it off so there's no cars. Tons of girls. Titties flashin'. It's great."

"That's cool, man."

"I'm Stevie," explained Stevie.

"Oh hey, I'm Mike." I held out my hand to shake his as he held out his fist to bump mine. So I closed my fist to bump as he opened his hand to shake. We oscillated greeting methods like this a few times before Stevie put an end to our manual dance.

"Just bump it, Mike." he said resolutely, and I complied. Then he said, "C'mon," and led me into a greenly lit convenience store so he could refill his Big Gulp with what I discovered was Malt Liquor.

"Beer is expensive at bars," Stevie reasoned as he emptied a 40 oz. bottle of Olde English into his plastic cup. I inquired about several tourist opportunities in Austin and Stevie responded enthusiastically. He ushered me up and down Sixth Street, my personal tour guide.

"That place always has good bands," he explained, "and on Tuesdays this place across the way has some seriously cheap drink specials. But the bouncers, they don't like me cause one time …they just …I was in there and like …I don't know. They're dicks. Cause you know me, Mike," in point of fact, I didn't know Stevie, had just met him, "I just try to get my drink on. This joint with the Christmas lights in the windows is a little bit more chill, mostly faggot-ass college kids. Oh, man, that place on the corner has some great ribs. They fall right off the bone. And the sauce, it's got a tang to it. You like tang? Hey, how 'bout some yayo? You want some coke?"

Cocaine with Stevie. I've done a lot of stupid things in my time. You're reading the writings of a man who has Netflixed Weird Al's U.H.F. nearly a dozen times and owes upwards of $15,000 to the I.R.S. I've been called reckless, irresponsible, and idiotic, mainly but not solely by my grandmother. However, at that moment it was difficult for me to conjure a scenario in which I'd do cocaine with Stevie and not end up broke and/or hospitalized.

"No, man, I don't know if I wanna do any coke," I said. "You know I'm only in Austin for a few days. I hear they got a great music scene here. I'd love to hear a blues band."

"You got it. We should probably find some weed first," replied Stevie, and he made a good point. A little pot seemed harmless when compared with the option of getting wantonly zooted on cocaine in a strange place with a strange Stevie.

Stevie led me to a bus stop just off Sixth Street, where a dozen or so Austinians awaited their various modes of transport. He told me his former cellmate would probably be waiting for his ride home from work.

"That's him," he said, indicating a man sleeping on a bench. Stevie walked over and jabbed the man in the shoulder. "Yo, Louie. Louie, get up, man."

"Hm? Oh, Stevie, what up, homes?" Louie groaned, stirring into consciousness. Louie's pink shirt hung on him like a hospital gown. Notable among his many tattoos was a great cannabis leaf stretching about his tawny neck that served to complement the few remaining jagged teeth in his mouth.

"Louie, do you got one of them little bags?" Stevie asked. "Me and Mike are gonna go see a band."

"Who's Mike?"

"Oh hey, how're you doing?" I said, reaching out my fist to bump Louie's. He didn't seem to notice.

"Is Mike a cop?" Louie asked Stevie. "Cause if he's a cop, he's gotta identify himself if I ask."

"He's not a cop," Stevie vouched for me.

"Are you a cop, Mike?" asked Louie, squinting at me. "Cause if you're a cop, you gotta identify yourself if I ask."

"I'm not a cop," I assured him.

"Okay. Cool, then, homes. You can never be too careful with white boys, you know," Louie explained. "But if you're a cop you gotta identify yourself if someone asks."

"Gotcha," I said.

"We're looking for some of them little bags," Stevie said, expediting the sale.

"Yeah, homes, how many do you need?"

"Just one." Stevie proceeded to buy a thin three-dollar bag of seeds, stems, and shake from Louie. He poured the entire contents of the bag into an EZ wide cigarette paper and tightened it up into a neat little joint, which he then lit and handed to me.

"Don't you think we should go to a more secluded spot with this?" I said, holding up the joint. We were, after all, still standing just off the heavily trafficked Sixth Street at a very public bus stop.

"It's okay," Stevie reassured me. "The only thing you gotta worry about is the cops." That's exactly what I was worried about.

"They'll fuck you here, man," Louie told me. "Texas cops

75

don't fuck around. Did you hear they executed this guy, and he was innocent, yo."

"No, I didn't hear that," I said.

"If a judge woulda heard his story, he woulda been innocent."

"A judge didn't hear his story?"

"No. Not enough time before they executed him. But he was innocent."

"Oh."

"It's fucked up, man."

Stevie interjected. "Mike's here from Pittsburgh."

"Philadelphia," I corrected, my head darting around, scanning for police. I desperately wanted the joint to burn faster. Not because the conversation wasn't scintillating, but because we were so exposed to law enforcement. I felt like a vacationer left behind in the open ocean when his cruise ship sailed away while he snorkeled. I expected a cop, like a shark, to jolt me from behind. The police could smell the tokes in the air like blood in the water, and I feared I would be caught unawares and out of my element.

"Right. Philadelphia," Stevie clarified.

"You're from Philadelphia? Do you know Rakim, um…" Louie searched his memory for a moment, "Rakim. I forget his last name. He works for the city."

"Hmmm… I'm not sure. Philly's a big place."

"Yeah. Fuckin' Eagles, right," Louie said, laughing.

"Hell yeah, man!" I answered.

"Yeah. I've seen them play Dallas. Did you see that game?" Louie asked.

"Um, they play Dallas twice every year," I said.

"Yeah. It was a good game."

To my relief, we finished the joint. Louie decided to forgo his bus ride home and joined Stevie and myself as we walked

76

to a blues bar.

"So guys, the first round is gonna be on me when we get to the bar," I said.

"Really?" asked Louie.

"Thanks, Mike," Stevie said through his constant grin.

"You guys are showing me around your city," I told them, beginning to cross the street. "And it's the least I can do. Austin's a pretty hospitable place. People have been good with giving me tips and directions. I got out to Barton Springs and walked the trail along the—"

Suddenly, Stevie yanked my arm backward. My heart blipped. My adrenaline surged. My head careened around looking for the car that must have been about to hit me. But there was no car. The street was empty.

"You want a ticket or something, Mike?!" Stevie asked as he pointed at the Don't Walk sign, the grin now gone from his face.

"Yeah, homes," Louie added, gravely. "Don't be jaywalkin' in Austin."

We hopped from bar to bar. We listened to this band and that band. We chugged beers. We downed shots. Stevie and Louie regaled me with tales of narcotic consumption, jail time, and illegitimate children. Stevie told me about how he supported his girlfriend's career ambitions by getting her an interview at a strip club. Louie showed me his stab wound. We cursed and howled and lied and laughed and peed in parking lots. But all the while, Stevie, Louie, and I crossed at the crosswalks.

MAGIC SKIN

Michael C. Keith

"Is not this a lamentable thing, that of the skin of an innocent lamb should be made parchment?"

— Shakespeare

Mbeya Road connected the village of Kisessa to the city of Mwanza. It was a patchwork of riven asphalt and rutted soil on which Huru Mohubi ran for his life as the moon drifted in and out of arid clouds. The stumps of the two fingers severed by the witch doctor's men throbbed but did not slow his flight to Mama Lweza. If he were caught, all of his body parts would be harvested and marketed to bring magical powers and instant wealth to others. Since his birth, Huru's bleached white skin had been a curse rather than a blessing—it certainly brought him no good fortune. Life as an albino had been a misery, and now at eighteen he was as close as he had ever come to being hacked to death because of the color of his flesh. While the white hippo was revered for its uniqueness, his human kind were feared and slaughtered because of their uncommon pigmentation.

Mama Lweza had saved his life before, as she had other African albinos, and if he could reach her, she would save him again. Her small brick and tin hut was perched on Lake

Ukerewe's edge on the northern fringe of Tanzania's second largest municipality. Stopping to catch his breath, Huru calculated that he must travel nine more kilometers to evade the fate his would-be butchers had in mind for him. There were five of them on his trail and at one point he could see their machetes as they caught the moon's beams. To Huru, they looked like a swarm of fireflies dancing on the dark horizon. As a boy he loved to collect the flashing insects in a jar and watch them blink on and off. Like him, they, too, were thought to possess magical powers, but unlike him, they were valued alive. So many times Huru wished he were a lightning bug, instead of a poor ghost boy.

"The Lord made you from fire as well. You are as the flying sparks ...a shining boy of the stars. So special on this earth, my sweet child," comforted Mama Lweza, who had cared for Huru after his parents abandoned him, fearing him possessed of the wicked shatani spirit.

At sixteen, Huru had left Mama Lweza's care to work alongside her brother Abasi in Kisessa, gathering sisal for rug makers. It was hard work, but Huru felt pride in supporting himself. Lweza's younger sibling was kind and defended him from villagers who mocked Huru when they went to market. When Darweshi, the local witch doctor, declared him the cause of a long drought, it became increasingly difficult for Huru to accompany Abasi to the center, so he would remain inside their modest hut until the older man returned. On two occasions, strangers had approached the hut while Huru was alone, but Abasi had returned in time to chase them away.

A month after the second encounter, Huru was finally abducted by the albino hunters and taken to the dwelling of Kisessa's prophet. It was there that Huru's fingers were lobbed off in order to be ground up and placed in amulets for sale to those that could afford their high price. The rest of his body would fetch millions of shillings, boasted the men that brought him to the witch doctor.

"An arm worth 100 thousand shillings. A foot 50 thousand, brothers," declared one of his captors, enthusiastically.

"Oh, but the ghost's head . . . it be worth 300 thousand!" shouted another, and they all cheered and swung their blades high in the air.

It surprised Huru that he was not chopped to death immediately. Instead he was deposited in a tiny shed next to the witch doctor's house. In the suffocating heat, he removed his shirt and wrapped it around the bloody remains of his right hand after attempting to cauterize the ragged incisions with a mixture of clay and saliva. He could hear the incantations of Darweshi and the cadenced responses of his assistants as the night deepened. Then silence followed, and Huru made his escape by tunneling under the thin Mukwa planks that comprised the leaning outbuilding. He was only a few hundred feet away when he heard voices shouting that he had disappeared.

"Look, I see the shadow of the ghost boy!" exclaimed someone from the direction of the oracle's compound.

At once, Huru knew he was in a race for his life, and he sprinted across the dusty terrain like the Masai tribesmen he had seen on the Serengeti. He felt he had extended the distance between himself and his predators only to realize they were within striking distance when he felt the sting of a rock against his bare shoulder. He left the road and zigzagged through a maze of shanties in an attempt to confuse his trackers.

"He has tricked us again with his black magic," observed one of the hunters, as Huru hid only a few feet from the group.

When they left the area, Huru set out as well, but with a new found determination to deprive them of their prized bounty. The words of Mama Lweza rang in his ears and gave him renewed purpose.

"You are different but that is what makes you one of the Lord's special children."

Huru quickly recalculated his course by locating the brightest star in the western sky. Unlike most albinos, his vision was unimpaired, and he used his good eyesight to his advantage all his young life. He now ran parallel to the road only using it when its shoulder became obstructed by rocks or fell away due to erosion. At his current pace, he figured he would reach Mama Lweza before the sun rose behind him and made his presence easier to detect by Darweshi's henchmen.

Huru's heart pounded harder when he arrived at the rim of the great lake, which meant that he was nearing his destination. He had not detected his pursuers in a while, and it increased his hope that he would reach Mama Lweza's shelter before they could catch him. As he moved up the hyacinth choked shoreline, two figures suddenly appeared from the brush. When he looked to his rear, he found two more men advancing toward him. As he was about to escape into the thicket, a fifth person emerged, and he knew he was trapped. The only open route left to him was the water, and Keeza could not swim. Still, he waded into the thick grassipes thinking he would rather drown than be hacked apart.

With each step Huru took into the lake, his stalkers moved closer to him, swinging their machetes and speaking in unison.

"No more evil ghost boy. No more devil tricks. We will take your powers."

Huru was waist deep in the water when a piercing metallic ring split the air and a brilliant light appeared from beneath the lake's surface. It was like a million fire flies were submerged a few feet from him.

"Devil come!" shouted the men surrounding him, who now stood frozen in fear.

A vast shining dome broke the surface, and a soft, beguiling voice beckoned Huru.

"Enter and be spared their swords. Live beyond their deeds. Come now," and he stepped inside the sphere of light.

Darweshi's huntsmen screamed and fell to the sand as the object shot into the air and vanished. Within the rapidly ascending object, Huru floated in a vacuum that relaxed him and made his eyelids heavy.

"Why do you take me?" he managed to whisper before succumbing to a deep sleep.

"Because you are special," replied a disembodied voice "A most rare Earthling."

In Huru's dream he held hands with dozens of fellow albinos in a field of orange and yellow azaleas, while Mama Lwesa led them in a popular Swahili song of exultation.

Eh Yakobo,
Eh Yakobo,
Walala?
Walala?
Amka twende Shule
Haya njoo,
Haya njoo,

After the first stanza, everyone began to sing, forming a wide circle and dancing. The once hostile villagers entered the field from all directions and joined the joyous activity, kissing and hugging the young albinos. Never before had Huru felt such happiness and love, and he awoke with tears of joy running down his cheeks to his ears. When he attempted to wipe them away, he found that his hands were secured to a table on which he lay. He then noticed his entire body was fastened to it as well.

"Why am I shackled?" he inquired, anxiously tugging at the restrains.

"You are special," replied a monotone voice.

"Why are these lines on my body?" asked Huru, surveying his torso as best he could, barely able to raise his head.

"We want your parts," came his answer.

Huru's screams were lost in the sounds of several swirling blades closing in on him from all directions.

PRAHA, CZECH REPUBLIC

Jeremy Rich

This catalyst country, a handful of split ends
Still gripped inverted by one leg
cry of freedom pending,
Communism still hangs a wet paint sign here

Cinereal cement clashes with scar worn cobblestone streets
That hum like quick zippers with passing cars
Even the clouds seem stiff and reflective of sound.

Echoes here are hard to pinpoint
Some ring the same in any language

An old woman yells to two teen daughters
Who linger long at the third story window
Her throat sandpapered raw
A guttural bellow
Of a different time

Feet heavy with intent
Thud back and forth across the ceiling
Walls rattle with force
Iron door slamming,
Shutting cold air outside

Bubbling cobblestone moat divides
But floorboards are not the only things that moan
Awake for work, with daylight still asleep
Tiptoeing sock-footed to the bathroom
At this hour between late arrivals and early risers
It continues.
Bodies pain for the warm weight of blankets
kissing black coffee they crane their necks

No translation needed
A cry crashes free
Bounces around shatters the ashen sky
softly glowing to embers

DENTED
Katherine Hinkebein

"Want to see the dent in my leg?"

Most people say yes when I ask that question, though it's probably more out of social courtesy than concern, or even curiosity. Then I volunteer to tell them how it got there. Once again, they're too polite to stop me. I wouldn't normally put people on the spot like that, but I find it fascinating—the dent, I mean—and I always think someday I'll run into someone who agrees with me.

So, this dent. It's in my left shinbone, maybe five inches above my ankle, and it's been there for just about three years. I got it while I was . . . I'm sorry, I just can't help myself. It's not even that good of a story; it's just one I like to tell. That's probably because it's about me, and because I have the evidence to prove it's true.

I think most people enjoy telling stories about themselves, certainly more than hearing someone else's story. It's the same with photographs. You might look carefully at a picture of other people, as long as you know them; if it's of people you don't even know, you probably skip right past it. But if it's a picture of yourself, you damn near memorize the thing. At least, that's what I do. I study every inch to make sure my hair is right, my teeth are clean, my eyes are open, and my face isn't frozen in some horrid contortion. It's narcissistic, but I bet you do it too.

When it comes to listening to other people's stories, it's generally only interesting if you're one of the characters. But when you're the one doing the telling, it's about seeing the audience's reaction. Are you funny, smart, interesting? Everyone likes a suspenseful narration of that night last year when you were followed and made a quick getaway just in the nick of time, or when you thought someone was breaking into your house last week but it turned out to be the cat . . . Comedy can be harder. If the story is only mildly entertaining, well, you get a polite grin and maybe a look of "why did you make me sit through that?" The really funny stories, however, those get the whole table laughing and then everyone is having fun, and the crowd likes you and the boys think you're cute, and isn't that the whole point?

Sounding smart is nice too, but no one likes a know-it-all, so it's better to go for clever.

Anyway, back to this dent in my leg. (I'll just tell part of the story, if that's all right.) I got it while I was staying in an RV in Austin for the summer. I was renting the RV from a guy who lived in it full time. Actually, that's a story unto itself. On a whim my friend invited me to come spend the summer with her in Austin, so I found a recreational vehicle for rent on craigslist and three weeks later I was driving from Missouri to Texas, ready to move in. The owner of this condo on wheels was headed to North Carolina and needed someone to "watch" it while he was away—for a small fee. Subletting was not allowed in the park, but he did want to make some money.

The RV was permanently situated in an RV park behind a Cuban restaurant, and it had a lean-to attached to the side of it with clear packing tape. The interior of the RV itself was about what you would expect: dirty brown carpet, a steering wheel at the front, a "kitchen" in the hallway, and at the back, a bedroom that fit a bed and nothing else. But the attached room, with its decent furniture, acceptable sunlight, and awesome stereo system, is where I spent most of my time. It even had Wi-Fi.

I stayed in Austin for seven weeks, although I wasn't in the RV that whole time. (Due to unforeseen events, some of which are relevant to this story, I moved roughly every two weeks, earning me the nickname of Gypsy Bitch.) It was a great experience. I and my friend—let's call her Kathy—had full-time jobs, but we managed to work those in around the drinking and eating and live music that filled our nights and weekends. With all that drinking and merrymaking, we ended up with some outrageous tales to tell.

Speaking of drinking stories, anyone over the age of eighteen has at least one. And if you're in the right crowd, trading those stories can last all night. Of course, after a while you have to preface your account with, "OK, don't think I'm an alcoholic or anything" before you can tell about the blurry two weeks you spent drunk and the one week you spent drying out. This is also where some real competition can come into play: who has the most outrageous, hideous, funny, puke your guts out drinking story? While the frosty beverages do seem to bring about some unbelievable events, the alcohol-soaked brain has a way of distorting the facts and exaggerating the smallest detail to epic proportions. And if you're drinking while telling your drinking stories (which is usually the case), the hyperbole knows no bounds.

But I wasn't drinking when I got the dent. (I was *getting ready* to go drinking, but that's clearly not the same thing.) I was standing in the shower, naked, just about to lather up. It was one of those tiny RV showers, which I had never experienced before, and it was tricky as hell. To get in, you had to lift the broken latch just right, step over the eighteen-inch-high doorframe into the four-foot-by-four-foot shower stall, latch the door again using your fingertips, and pull the curtain closed. The actual showering was just as complicated. To keep the hot water from running out, I was instructed to take a "navy shower." That meant turn on the water, get wet, turn off the water, lather up, turn on the water, rinse off and wet my hair, turn off the water, lather up the shampoo, turn on the water, rinse off. Just imagine what it was like when I tried to shave my legs!

It's too bad movies never make use of the RV shower. What if the most famous of all shower scenes had taken place in an RV? That would have been something. I mean, it would have given a whole different feel to that movie. Norman Bates could have run this remote RV park where he lived with his mother in a silver Airstream, and it was the close quarters that drove him to murder. Everyone knows people who grow up in RV parks are predisposed to criminal behavior, so it really wouldn't be that much of a stretch. And if Lila had been driving a double-wide when she was escaping with that bag of money, it would have been much more exciting than the getaway in her little sedan. I wonder if Hitchcock considered having Lila shave her legs during that scene in the shower. The razor would have come in handy.

But I wasn't shaving my legs when I got this dent. I didn't make it that far. (Since I've told you this much, mind if I just fill in the rest?) I was standing in the shower and had completed the first two steps—"turn on the water and get wet"—in the navy shower ritual. As I reached for the soap I must have knocked the curtain, because a giant living cockroach fell from the ceiling, grazed my shoulder, and bounced onto the shower floor! I screamed! Mashing myself up against the wall, I struggled to draw back the curtain and undo that tricky latch

89

while *la cucaracha* menacingly crawled around on the wet floor. I was in such a hurry to get away from the awful creature that when the door finally swung open, I leaped out of that would-be coffin without stepping over the eighteen inches of metal that separated the shower from the hall. In so doing, my shin crashed into the doorframe and my foot followed suit. When it was all done, I was naked, wet, spread out on the RV's filthy shag rug, and after a moment, crying.

With a couple of deep breaths, I got myself together, wrapped a towel around my body, then called Kathy for help. In a pathetic, anguished voice I said, "I hurt my leg real bad." Being the excellent friend that she is, Kathy replied with "I'll be right there," and left work to come to my aid. Shortly after I hung up, I realized I had not broken the bone, but it didn't look good. Kathy helped me get ice on my leg, then very gently loaded me into her car. Less than twenty minutes after the accident I was at her house, finishing my shower so we could get on with our night's entertainment: the bar. I had been in town for just shy of two weeks, and that was the last night I spent in the RV.

Unfortunately, all the ice in the world wasn't going to help that injury. For days my shin was swollen and purple, and the top of my foot was one giant bruise. The gross part came when the blood from the bruise in my shin began to spread down my leg to my ankle. That's what weak blood vessels will do for you. At least I have strong bones. Nothing was broken, but my tibia has never fully healed.

And that's how I got this dent in my leg. Wanna see?

THE LAST ELECTION

Frank Roger

The torches cast a flickering light on the handful of men huddled in the shelter. One of them cleared his throat, raised his hand to catch everyone's attention and said:

"I really think we should go ahead with the election. There's just no time to lose."

A second man nodded and replied:

"I can see your point, but don't you think it will be just a symbolical event? Don't we need more than symbols at this stage? Those earthquakes virtually destroyed the entire planet, and swept away human civilisation. Will that election really help us?"

For a moment there was silence as they were all lost in thought. Then a third man said in a quiet voice:

"Well, I suppose there's an end to everything. As far as we know we're all that's left of humanity. And how much time do we have left? Our supplies are running out, and when we leave this shelter we'll meet sudden death outside. Admit it, guys, it's over for us. This is the end of the line. Still, that doesn't mean there's no point in honouring important traditions up until the very last moment. I tend to agree with our friend's proposal. We should go ahead with the election. We can't go on without a representative of God on earth, even if there's only a handful of faithful followers left."

"But I'm just a priest. Only a cardinal can be elected as the new pope. And with all due respect, you're not cardinals either, so you're not allowed to vote."

All the men waved his protests away.

"You're the only candidate for the papacy. And we're all devout believers. Considering the seriousness of our current situation, I'd say we should allow for some leniency. Let's go ahead with it. This is too important to cancel because of technical details."

"Technical details," the candidate for the papacy muttered, shaking his head.

"The Church has been without a leader for too long. And when we die, it will be too late. This is no way for Christianity or humanity to end. Let's act quickly. I know the procedure takes time, but we should speed it up. We've wasted enough time as it is."

They conferred a final time, and mere minutes later the votes were cast. Unsurprisingly, the priest was informed he had been elected as the new pope, in all probability the very last one in line.

One of the men held a moist cloth next to a torch, and white smoke billowed up that made everyone cough. When they were able to breathe again, someone said hoarsely: "Habemus papam."

The newly elected pope rose to his feet, clearly overwhelmed by emotion.

"I thank you all for this great honour," he said. "I'm afraid that I'm at a loss for words."

"You need to take a name," someone reminded him.

The pope nodded, thought for a moment and announced: "I inform you that I take the name of Paul VIII. May God bless you all."

They all erupted into cheers and applauded him.

"The Vatican is gone," someone cried out, "but the Catholic Church is still alive, the Catholic faith still lives on, and there is still a representative of God on earth."

"New York, Paris, London, Rome, it's all gone, swept away, but we keep the flame of Christianity burning. May God bless us all!" another one joined in.

"Humanity's almost wiped out by the cataclysm, but we will carry on until the very end, sustained by our faith, and protected by God."

Pope Paul VIII looked at his disciples and nodded. "There's just a handful of us left, and we may not have much more time. Let us now…"

A quake hit the shelter, and the men desperately looked for cover as part of the roof caved in, and debris and dust made it almost impossible to breathe. The torches went out too, and blackness surrounded them.

"Are you all right?" a voice finally came from the darkness. What was left of the roof came down, and when the dust had settled they could see the stars and a crescent moon overhead, spreading just enough light to make out vague silhouettes.

"I'm okay. Did all of us make it?"

It turned out only three of them were still alive, and the newly elected Pope was not among them.

"Pope Paul VIII is dead," one of them lamented. "Mere moments after his election. How tragic."

"It was the shortest pontificate in the history of the Catholic Church," the second survivor commented.

"This just has to be a sign of God," the third man wailed. "We must have failed him. The Pope was struck down by God's hand. And look at that crescent moon. The symbol of the Islam! God is mocking us!"

"Don't be silly," the first man reprimanded him. "You must have been hit on the head by a rock just there."

"Kill the heretic," the second man screamed. "We're all that's left of humanity, of the Catholic community. Let's keep our faith pure!"

The two men went for each other's throat, and the sole spectator shouted: "Stop that! Think of the commandments! God's children don't fight, and they certainly don't kill. Behave yourselves. We're probably the last human beings still alive on the planet. Let's spend the time we're still granted here in dignity."

The two others suddenly screamed with panic as they disappeared into a crevice they hadn't seen in the semi-darkness, and the only remaining man on earth stood pondering.

Well, he thought, I must have reached the end of the line. I'm the final witness of the apocalypse. All I can do is wait until my maker calls me back.

He sat down and meditated until an idea struck him. What if I hold another election, he thought. This is my chance to become God's representative on earth. Now obviously I'm the only candidate, and I'm also the only one able to cast a vote. It would be wholly symbolical. On the other hand, why pass up this chance? This is my opportunity to become Paul IX. Or perhaps John Paul IV. Or what about Pius XIII? Benedictus XVII?

He still hadn't decided on a name as another quake made him roll down the slope, thus abruptly finishing his papal ambitions, as well as humanity's reign over the planet.

IN PANAMA
William Doreski

Your rear deck abuts the canal
so closely I can stretch to touch
the flanks of huge container ships
creeping along with Chinese goods
piled six boxes tall on deck.
The climate's so lush your garden
looks nubile as flesh. Prowling
amid the squash and lettuce you smile
that famous oyster of a smile
and I want to roll in the soil
and howl with all of my organs.

We like Panama—the government
too timid to annoy us
despite the khaki uniforms,
the tourists sobered by the sight
of the canal with its massive
steel and concrete locks receiving
hulking black-hulled ships with ease.
I like to spend the days reading
on the deck and waving at crews
from every nation in the world.
You with your garden obsession

so tire yourself that by evening
while I peel and cook vegetables
for yet another casserole
you lie so flat on your chaise-longue
you look like a paper doll.

At night the canal smells deep
as the world's great lobotomy.
The Atlantic and Pacific meet
reluctantly, at different levels.
Why can't the oceans lie as flat
as you can? We slip into bed
like big freighters into the locks
and every day we emerge fresh
in the lukewarm view and peer
up and down the canal to count
the ships the way Homer did,
the stream of commerce brimming.

LIAR, LIAR
Aida Zilelian

Growing up, my sister Alice and I were forbidden to watch most shows on television. My foreign-born mother felt that it would Americanize us—a dilemma that she would constantly battle throughout most of our lives. She also quickly realized that I absorbed the infamous quips of any sitcom that I was even briefly exposed to. I had a tendency of repeating these lines at any given chance, and she perceived herself as the ultimate victim of humiliation if we were to go somewhere public. If we were at the supermarket and she refused to buy me a box of Lucky Charms cereal, I would counter loudly with, "What'chu talkin' 'bout, Willis?" Or if she casually picked up a box of Jell-O pudding pops from the frozen food aisle I would exclaim, "Dyn-O-MITE!" Most mothers would have cooed over my cute and clever delivery. But mother found this behavior insolent and overall disgusting. Therefore, we spent the majority of our time listening to old albums that had been collected by the family over the years. These, too, I mimicked, and I memorized songs with a startling ease that was coupled with the willingness to sing at any given opportunity.

The summer I was eleven and my sister Alice was six my mother decided to send us to CYO day camp, in an effort to keep our minds active and occupied. It was the 80's. "Eye of the Tiger" was constantly blasting from the huge boombox in the back of a very muggy school bus where all the counselors sat together. The girls wore satin shorts with white trimming and snug-fitting day camp T-shirts. The guys also wore the same thing, but they smoked cigarettes that were safely tucked in their tube socks, which were pulled up to their knees with a dangerous assuredness. The smell of Hubba Bubba permeated the air. The tan leather seats stuck to the backs of my knees and made a suction cup sound every time I repositioned my legs.

And all the while, as I sat there looking through the window, marveling at the row of trees that neatly followed one after the other, various tunes would hum through my head. While waiting for the camp school bus to pick us up, I would sit outside of the house on the lawn and provide all of 113th St, my sister Alice and anyone else who was willing to listen, with the entire Annie soundtrack. I had eleven years of experience sitting in front of a record player and its crackling needle, which provided me with lovely melodies from musicals such as "My Fair Lady" and "Gigi", to name a few. I deviated from this, of course, during my mother's once a week cleaning schedule, which was punctuated with the "Guilty" album featuring Barbara Streisand and Barry Gibb.

One particular afternoon the counselors and campers are changing into their clothes after swimming in the pool. I am standing in a large bathroom with the rest of them, trying unsuccessfully to braid my long brown hair with the same precision that my mother demonstrated that very morning. I'm humming "Tomorrow" to myself a bit too loudly, and it catches the attention of one of the more gullible and unsuspecting counselors. When she asks me what song I'm humming, I try to hide my glee and push down a triumphant smile.

"I'm just practicing," I say, and continue humming, having no idea where I plan on taking this.

"Practicing for what?" she asks, and it takes every ounce of self-control to suppress the hysterical giggle rising in my throat.

"I'm not supposed to say anything to anyone. My mom told me people would make a big deal about it," I answer with a whisper and pretend to fidget with my braids.

"Oh, you know I won't say anything! Why don't you tell me?" she urges.

I feign hesitation for a brief moment, displaying a visible struggle between my mother's instructions and telling Jynell, this bony-kneed, metal-mouthed goof, my alleged secret.

"Well," I begin, eyes darting from one corner of the room to the other, "do you know the play Annie'?"

Jynell nods anxiously.

"I auditioned for it two weeks ago. And I got the part. I'm going to star as Little Orphan Annie."

Despite the painfully failing resemblance between myself, a brown-haired, brown-eyed Armenian—with olive skin, no less—and Little Orphan Annie, all confidentiality between Jynell and myself was forever lost.

She whirls around and jumps up and down, yelling, "Guess what, everyone?! She's going to be in Annie!" and points at me. After a few more of these exclamations, everyone stops talking and the room is quiet.

Jynell looks pleased to the point where she might as well have been the casting director.

"Aida, why don't you sing us something?" she says, standing behind me with her hands on my shoulders.

"I don't know what to sing," I say, looking down at the floor, forming figure eight shapes with the toe of my sandal. I look up and everyone is waiting with a quiet expectation. This was the first time in my life I had the full attention of an entire room full of people, and I wasn't about to fuck it up.

"Whatever you were singing before," Jynell says, standing behind me and squeezing my shoulders with reassurance.

"Okay," I say, and take two steps forward.

I clear my throat and look around the room. I begin singing my rendition of "Tomorrow." My hands begin to move with emotion, and for the few moments that I unclench my eyes, I see two-dozen watching me. Looking back, I have no idea if I was any good, but when I finished, they all clapped with awe. Had I sung "I'm a little tea pot" I would have inspired the same reaction; it was my bravado that had been impressive. The point was: I was a star on Broadway. And, after that day, for a week or two, I was treated with a quiet reverence. I, too, was convinced of my impending fame, until it was all forgotten, as most things are once the novelty fades.

Unlike myself, my younger sister Alice lied in the opposite fashion: she withheld information instead of inventing it. This, coupled with our mother's deep-seated penchant turned one particular afternoon into an interrogation. If it wasn't exhausting enough for our mother to fulfill her parental obligations of guiding and reprimanding Alice and I, my mother had also assumed the tireless role of the household private detective. Never was a diary, notebook, or letter read with the stealth and enthusiasm that my mother graciously exhibited during all the years I lived with her. I should have been flattered. She was my number-one fan. No one in this world has read as much of my writing as she has. And although my master's thesis sat on her night table collecting dust for ten months and was ultimately left unread, I know this was only because she was more attached to the material I had produced in my formative years. No, she was no snob. She didn't like the fuss of big words and fancy grammatically correct sentences.

My sister Alice would also agree about our mother's

detrimental snooping habit. When I was younger, I would hide the usual accoutrements that most teenagers did: a pack of cigarettes, black eyeliner, a diary, and perhaps one of my mother's lipsticks. But Alice would hide her underwear. This random and puzzling phenomenon enraged my mother one afternoon while she was doing the laundry and realized that none of Alice's underwear was in the hamper.

As an aside, I feel it necessary to emphasize the importance of underwear in our household. I suppose it is best to say that my mother was the underwear Kommandant. Not only was the number of underwear regulated (i.e. we each had fourteen pairs), but the frequency of how often we changed them was also monitored, and she would remember to ask us at the most unforeseen moments. Sometimes during a car ride to school, or when we were sitting in a Burger King for lunch, she would lean over, make eye contact with both of us, and whisper (in Armenian) "Did you change your underwear today?" If this systematic scrutiny were not enough, we were only to wear one type: white underwear that if you pulled up, would safely meet your bellybutton. This mandatory dress code went unquestioned and practically unnoticed until Alice dared to walk to the local Woolworth and return with a six-pack of dark purple and fuchsia underwear. Aside from being an irresponsible oversight, my mother wanted to know: how did Alice expect her to wash them? As if all our clothes were white and there was no pile of dark laundry that this defenseless underwear could've been thrown into. Poor Alice. Any aspirations of breaking away from this enforced uniform were quickly dissolved.

One afternoon Alice and I were sitting in her bedroom shoving chocolate in our mouths. Chocolate was doled out sparingly in our household, and Alice had stolen the Godiva box that was reserved for guests out of the liquor cabinet and had scrambled into her room. The door flew open and there we were with chocolate stuffed in our mouths and raspberry crème oozing from our chins.

"Where is your underwear?" my mother yelled. In addition to her high-pitched, gypsy-like screaming, my mother's accent has been a source of amusement for my cousins and myself for as long as I can remember. She rolls her r's and replaces any 'th' sound with a 'd'. Once I realized that this was the formula for imitating her, it was like learning to speak a new language with little effort, and impressing dozens upon dozens of listeners.

Alice gazed up at my mother, unable to answer.

"Where is your underwear?"

"I don't know," she mumbled, without swallowing.

"You don't know. Where. Is. Your. Underwear?"

"I lost it."

I looked down at the floor, trying to fixate on something fascinating. The scene I was anticipating would be too much to bear.

My mother pursed her lips, grabbed both of us by the arm, and flung us out of the room, with chocolate spewing out of our mouths. We sat on the floor and pressed our ears against the door, listening to drawers being opened and slammed shut, closets being rummaged through. I looked at Alice and she said nothing. She reminded me of a Little House on the Prairie episode when this new mute girl was introduced to the class in Walnut Grove. When all the children said, "Hello Myra!", the mute girl just looked blankly at the floor and didn't answer in return. I suppose Alice's mind was worrying over the party in the courtyard that afternoon. She had been looking forward to seeing her friends all week, and the weather was perfect. Suddenly we heard the crackle of a plastic bag and the door slowly opened.

"Aida, stay outside. Alice, get in here."

I stood up and walked to the other side of the apartment, where my mother's sharp voice was betrayed by the acoustics of the room. "...and that's it! No more garden party for you! I ask you: where is your underwear. What do you say to me? You lost it? Here it is! Here it is!" and I heard the aggravated shaking of the plastic bag. "No more! Finish! No garden party!" and the door flew open with my mother stomping down the hallway. When she had disappeared into the laundry room I peeked my head in and saw Alice sobbing in the corner. A few minutes later my mother returned less perturbed, and walked into Alice's room.

"Okay, I have an idea," she said calmly. Alice sat in the corner of the room in her newfound stupor.

"Alice, I have an idea," my mother said more firmly. Again there was no response.

"Alice! I have an idea!" she screamed, and Alice jumped as if jolted from her trance.

"You can go to the party," she said, lowering her voice again, "but under one condition: you have to wear a sign on your neck."

"A sign?" Alice croaked. It was the first word she'd uttered for an hour.

"Yes, a sign," my mother said, trying to sound reasonable.

"What sign?"

"The sign has to say, 'Liar'. I will make it for you. You hang it on your neck and wear it, and then you can go to the party," my mother finished, in a tone conveying the impression that she felt this was a fair and acceptable term of agreement.

Needless to say, Alice preferred to stay indoors instead of parading around the courtyard to display her shameful logo of dishonesty. Instead, she sat in front of the window that overlooked the courtyard and watched her friends play in the sun, where they occasionally waved at her, ultimately unmoved by her incarceration.

CONTRIBUTORS

Born in New York but long a resident in Paris, HOWARD WALDMAN taught European History for a France-based American university and later American Literature for a French University. His short stories have appeared in Verbsap, Gold Dust, Global Inner Visions, and other publications. He has published four novels, all available on Amazon: *Back There, Time Travail, The Seventh Candidate,* and *Good Americans Go to Paris When They Die.*

PHIL SMITH III is a Mainframe Architect at Voltage Security, an enterprise software vendor. He grew up in a "literary" family, with a linguist father and a polymath mother, and cannot remember a family dinner when the dictionary was not consulted at least once. (This might sound boring, but given his parents' encyclopedic knowledge of words, anything that needed looking up was guaranteed to be something interesting!) Phil has spent over 30 years doing and managing software support/development. He also creates technical reference books, writes for trade journals, speaks at national and local computer user groups, and tracks IBM evolution. Occasionally, he finds time to write a little fiction.

TIM CONLEY's last book was *Whatever Happens* (Insomniac Press, 2006), which was shortlisted for the Re Lit Award. The story submitted here is part of the next collection he's putting together. For better or worse, he lives in St. Catharines, Ontario (Canada).

JACK FREY is a Canadian who lives in Beijing, China, with his wife and two young boys. He finds the letter K to be the most aesthetically pleasing of all the consonants, in both its upper and lowercase forms. Bits of his work have appeared or are forthcoming in Shelf Life Magazine, Writers' Bloc (Rutgers), Fractured West, and The Last Man Anthology, among others. Like many of us, he is currently working on his first novel. (http://jackfrey.wordpress.com)

MICHAEL C. KEITH is the author of numerous books, articles, and stories. He teaches communication at Boston College. (www.michaelckeith.com). His story collection *Hoag's Object* will be published by Whiskey Creek Press.

FRANK ROGER is a Belgian short story writer with a few hundred stories to his credit and publications in more than 30 languages.

LAURY A. EGAN's two full-length poetry collections, *Snow, Shadows, a Stranger* (2009) and *Beneath the Lion's Paw* (2011), were published by FootHills Publishing. Her work has received nominations for a Pushcart Prize, Best of the Web, and Best of the Net, and has appeared in Atlanta Review, Welter, The Emily Dickinson Awards Anthology, The Ledge, Centrifugal Eye, Willows Wept Review, Diverse Voices Quarterly, Boston Literary Magazine, Lowestoft Chronicle, Best of Foliate Oak 2010, and other journals. In addition, she writes fiction and is a fine arts photographer. Web site: www.lauryaegan.com

DAVIDE TRAME is an Italian teacher of English, born and living in Venice, Italy, writing poems exclusively in English since 1993. They have been published in around five hundred literary magazines since 1999, in U.K, U.S., and elsewhere. His poetry collection, *Re-Emerging*, was published as an on-line book by www.gattopublishing.com in 2006.

LISA ABELLERA is a writer living in the San Francisco Bay Area. She has recently completed her MFA in Creative Writing at the University of San Francisco. She is currently working on a collection of short stories. This is her first poetry publication.

JEREMY RICH is an 8th grade Language Arts teacher in Colorado. His poetry has appeared in Watershed, Take Back The Night, Chantarelle's Notebook, Ceremony, Thick with Conviction, Speedpoets, Poetic Hours, as well as various other print and online journals.

WILLIAM DORESKI teaches at Keene State College in New Hampshire. His most recent collection of poetry is *Waiting for the Angel* (2009). He has published three critical studies, including Robert Lowell's Shifting Colors. His essays, poetry, fiction, and reviews have appeared in many journals, including Massachusetts Review, Atlanta Review, Notre Dame Review, The Alembic, New England Quarterly, Harvard Review, Modern Philology, Antioch Review, and Natural Bridge.

ERIC G. MÜLLER is a musician, teacher and writer. He has written two novels, *Rites of Rock* (Adonis Press, 2005) and *Meet Me at the Met* (Plain View Press, 2010), as well as a collection of poetry, *Coffee on the Piano for You* (Adonis Press, 2008), and numerous short stories that have been published here and there. www. ericgmuller.com

While science fiction is BRINNA DEAVELLAR's first love, humor is a close second. She is an avid reader of fiction of all genres and non-fiction on such topics as sociology and medicine. Her work has appeared in the e-zine M-Brane SF.

Since Tyke Johnson can't live up to the expectations of Christ, he does his best to live up to the expectations of his dentist. So far, no cavities. He's been published by The Los Angeles Review, Ducts, Opium Magazine, and Unlikely Stories 2.0, among others. He lives in Los Angeles California where everyone complains about the parking at Trader Joe's.

Michael Connor is a humorist from Philadelphia who studied English Literature and Film at Oberlin College. His work has appeared in Hot Psychology Magazine and Examiner.com. He has written numerous comedic pieces for the stage including the musical The Hoppers Hit the Road. In addition, Mike has performed stand-up and improv comedy throughout the country, and can be seen regularly with the comedy troupe the N Crowd.

Katherine Hinkebein, owner of P.O.P. Editorial Services, has been an editor for more than ten years. She has had three other essays published with the online magazine Keepgoing.org. She lives in St. Louis, Missouri.

Aida Zilelian's work has been featured in Pen Pusher (UK), SN Review, Visions, Slushpile, Wilderness House Literary Review, Suss: Another literary journal, The Fertile Source, and most recently Halfway Down the Stairs.

Jennine Capó Crucet was born to Cuban parents and raised in Miami, Florida. Her debut book, *How to Leave Hialeah*, won the Iowa Short Fiction Prize, the John Gardner Award, and was named a Best Book of the Year by the Miami Herald. She's the recipient of the Winthrop Prize & Residency for Emerging Writers, the Devil's Kitchen Reading Award in Prose, and scholarships to the Bread Loaf Writers' Conference. She's been a finalist for both the Missouri Review Editor's Prize and the Latino Literary Prize. Her stories have appeared in Ploughshares, Epoch, Gulf Coast, the Southern Review, The Los Angeles Review, and other magazines. She currently divides her time between Miami and Los Angeles, and lives online at www.jcapocrucet.com

TOM MAHONY is a biological consultant in California, with an M.S. degree from Humboldt State University. His fiction has been nominated for a Pushcart Prize and has appeared in dozens of online and print publications, including Surfer Magazine, Flashquake, The Rose & Thorn, Pindeldyboz, In Posse Review, Boston Literary Magazine, 34th Parallel, Diddledog, Foliate Oak, and DecomP. His first novel, *Imperfect Solitude*, was published by Casperian Books in 2010. Visit him at tommahony.net.

RON D'ALENA was born in San Francisco, earned an MBA at the University of San Francisco, and now lives in Southern Oregon with his wife and son. Since 2008, his work has appeared or is forthcoming in numerous journals and magazines including Slipstream, Underground Voices Anthology 2009, Johnny America, Reed Magazine, Big Lucks, EDGE, and Criminal Class Review. He is a two-time Glimmer Train Finalist and nominee for the 2012 Pushcart Prize for fiction.

COPYRIGHT NOTES

CPSIA information can be obtained at www.ICGtesting.com
Printed in the USA
LVOW06s1516051113

360105LV00002B/537/P